When LLAMA learns to LISTEN

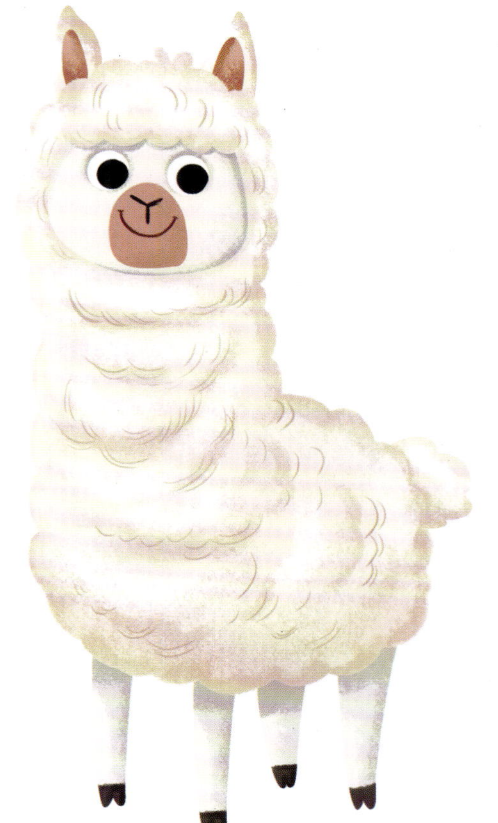

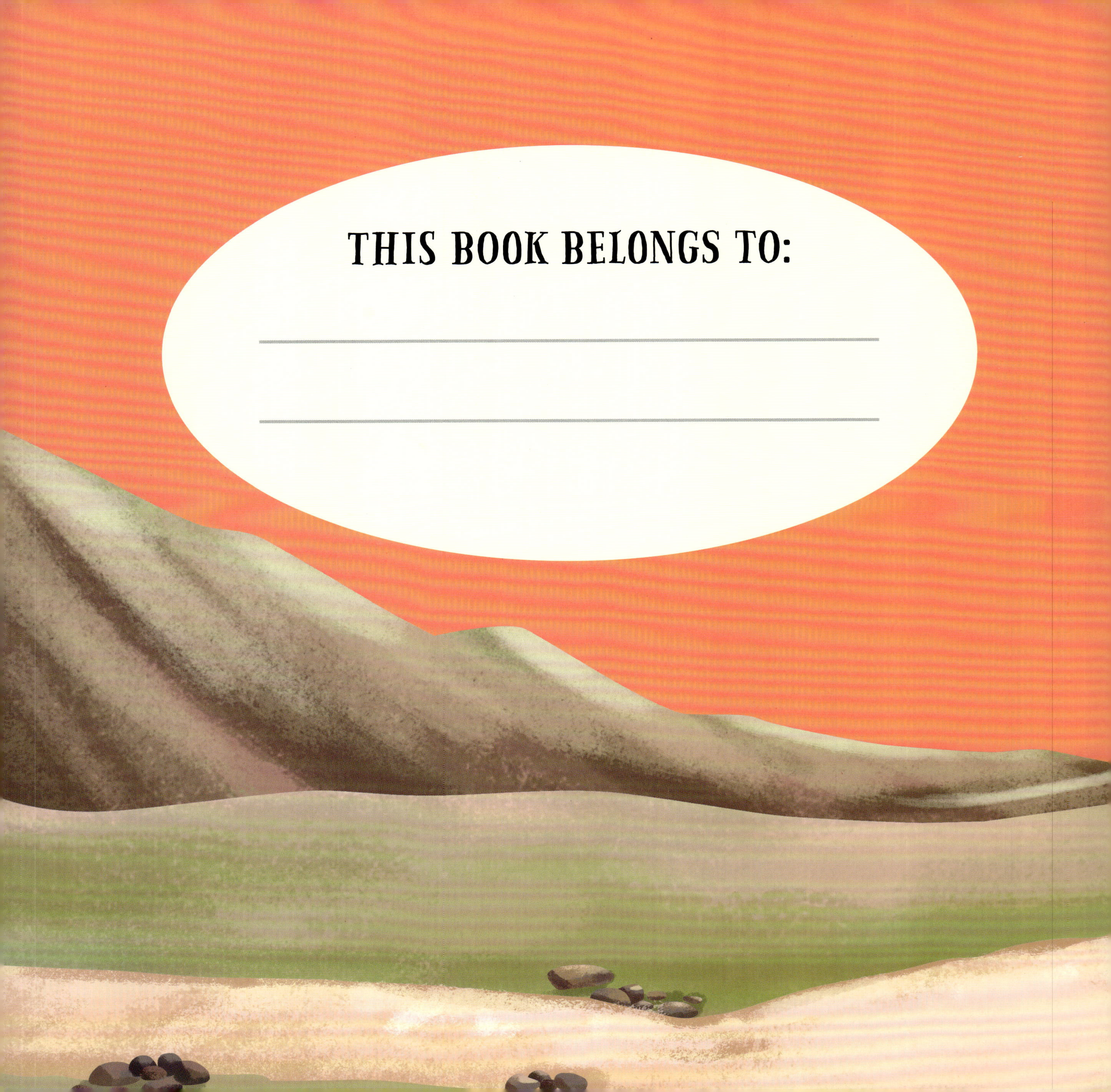

THIS BOOK BELONGS TO:

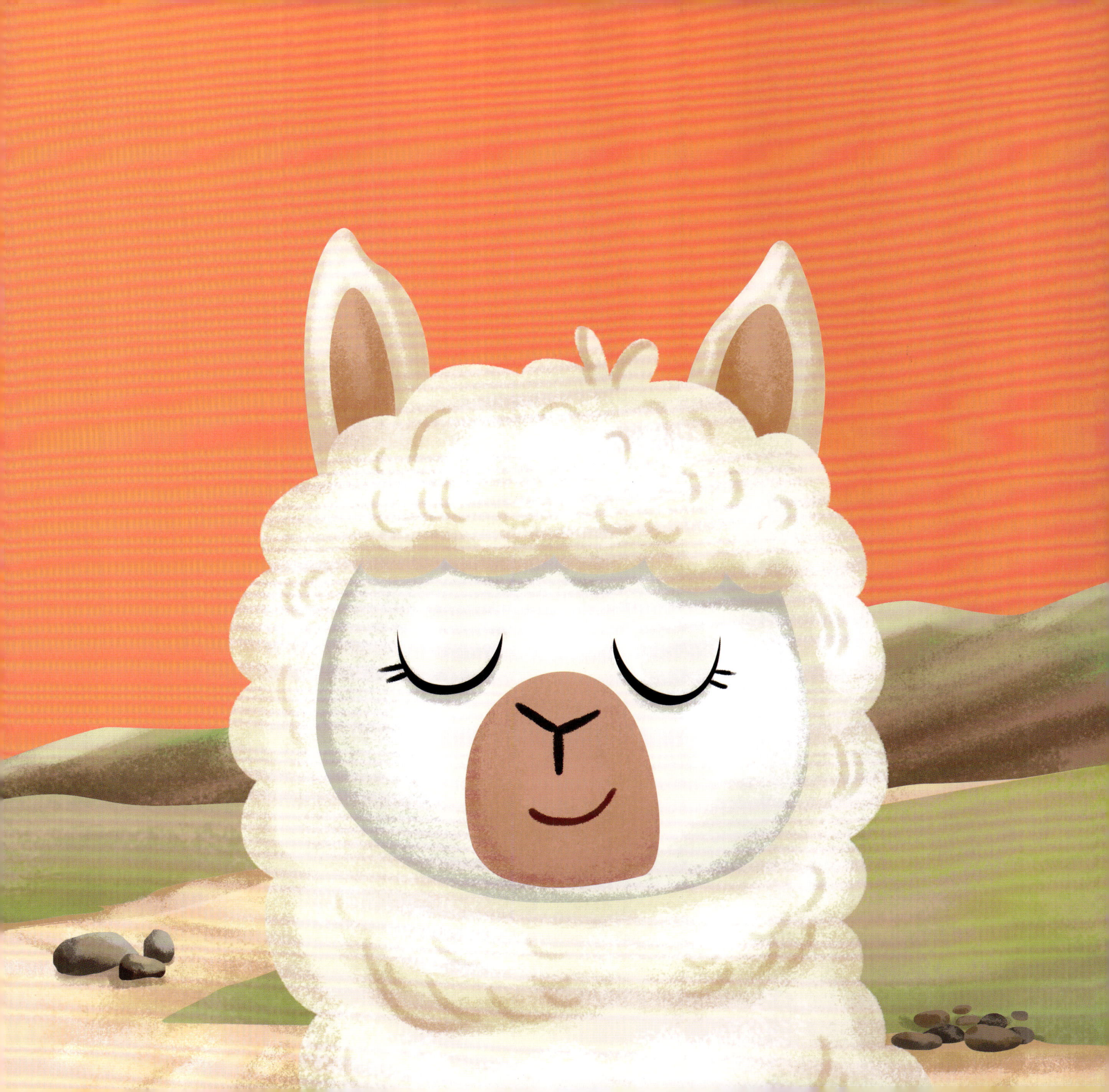

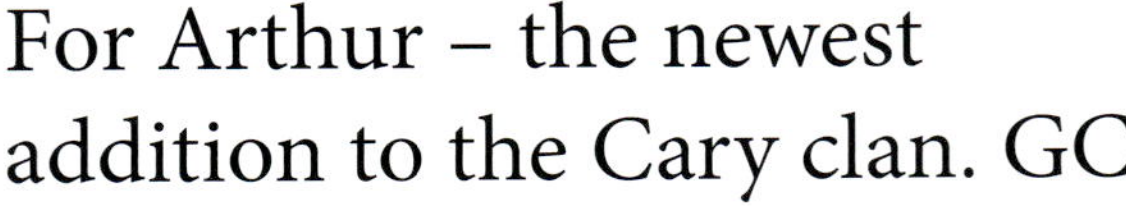

For Arthur – the newest
addition to the Cary clan. GC

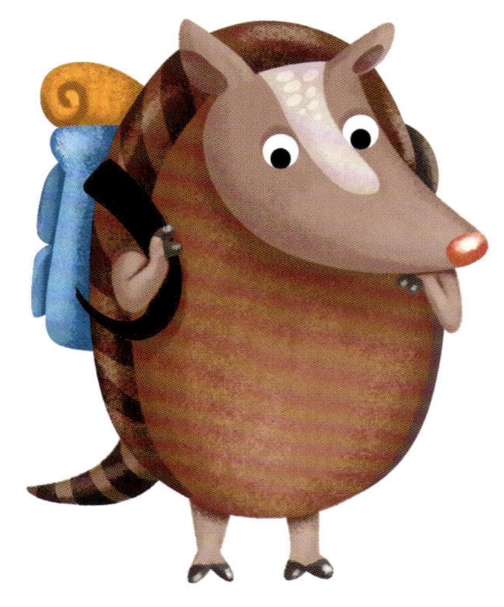

First published in 2025 by North Parade Publishing

North Parade Publishing Ltd
3-6 Henrietta Mews,
Bath UK
BA2 6LR

www.nppbooks.co.uk

This edition is printed in 2025 exclusively for
WS Pacific Publications, Inc.
Manila, Philippines
www.learningisfun.com.ph

ISBN 978-1-83923-798-0

Printed and bound in China.

When LLAMA learns to LISTEN

Gemma Cary

Krishna Kumar

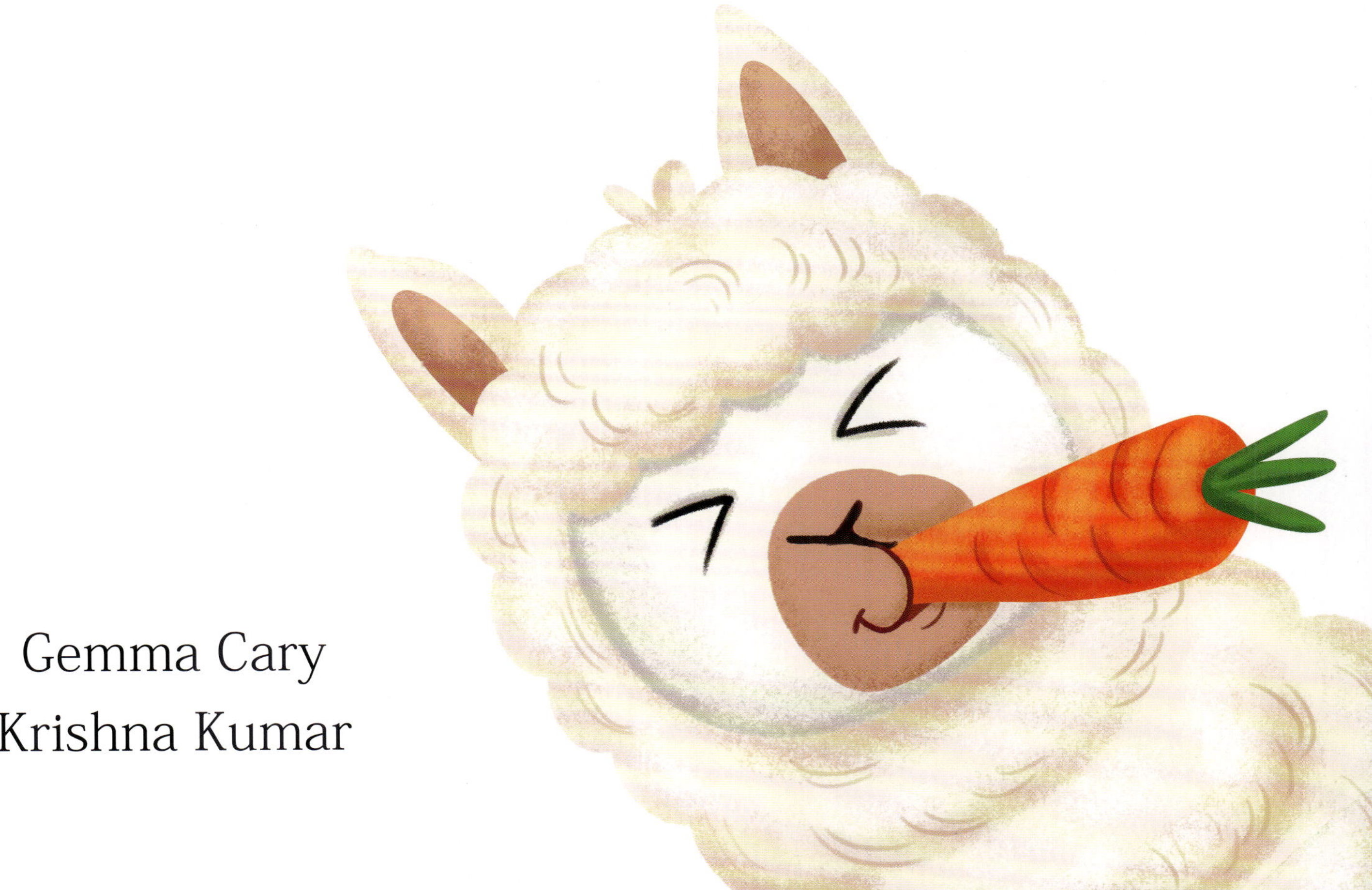

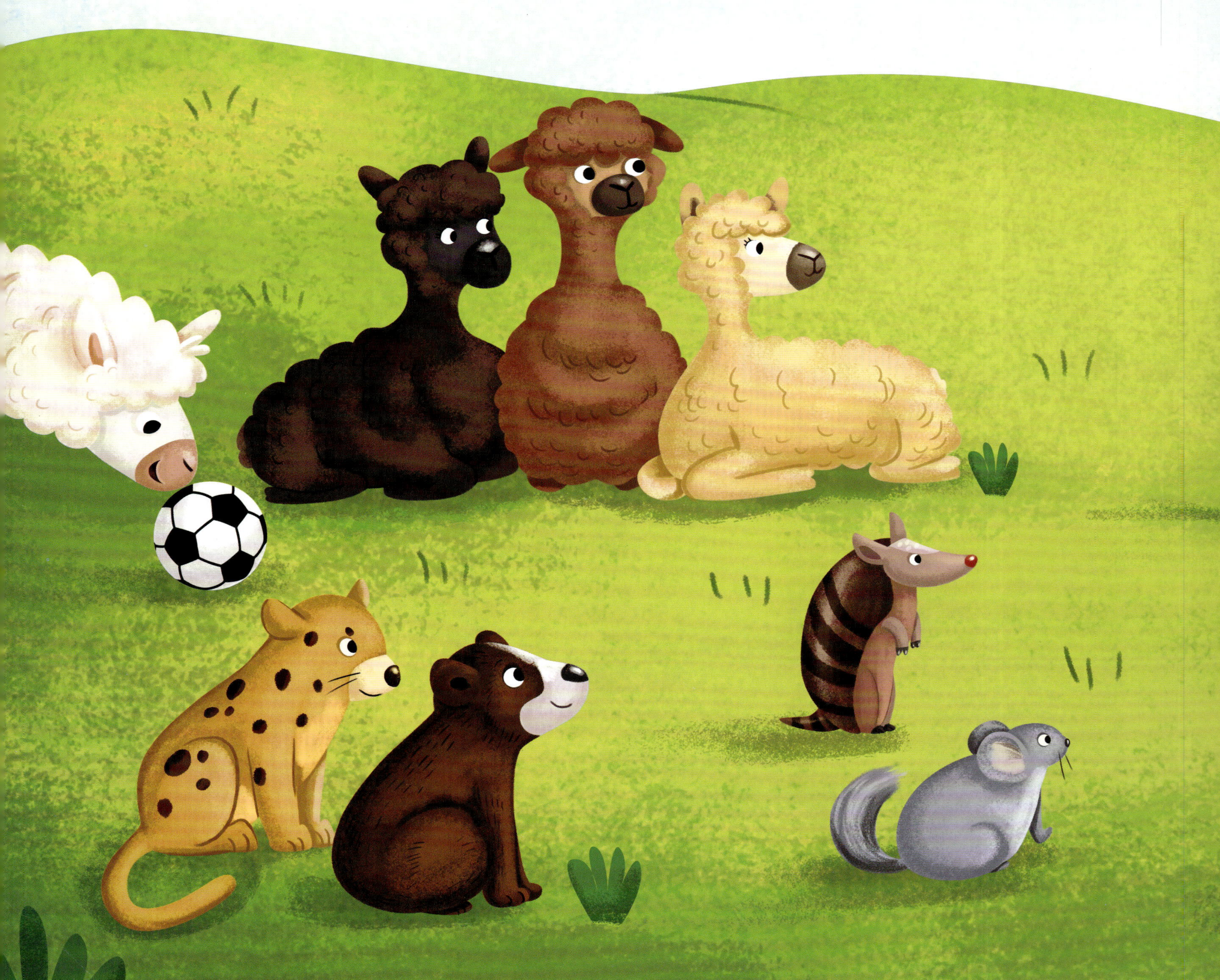

Deep down in the valley, a teacher calls his class.
He asks them all to gather in the **long, cool** grass.

"Children!" he begins, with a **smile** across his face.
"Tomorrow we are going to a very **special** place.
You may wish to bring walking boots – and possibly a hat.
But **don't forget** to pack a lunch, some water and a snack."

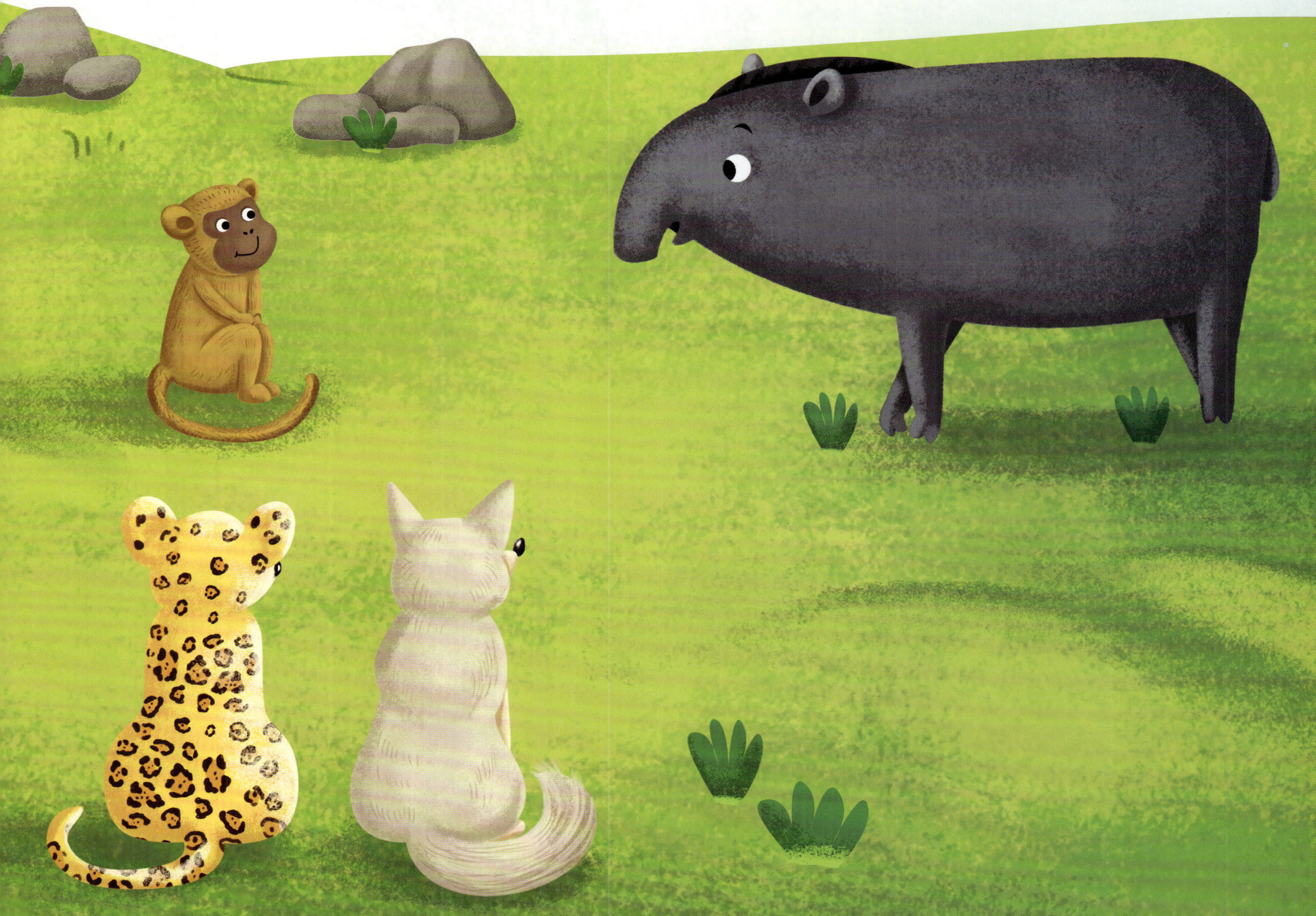

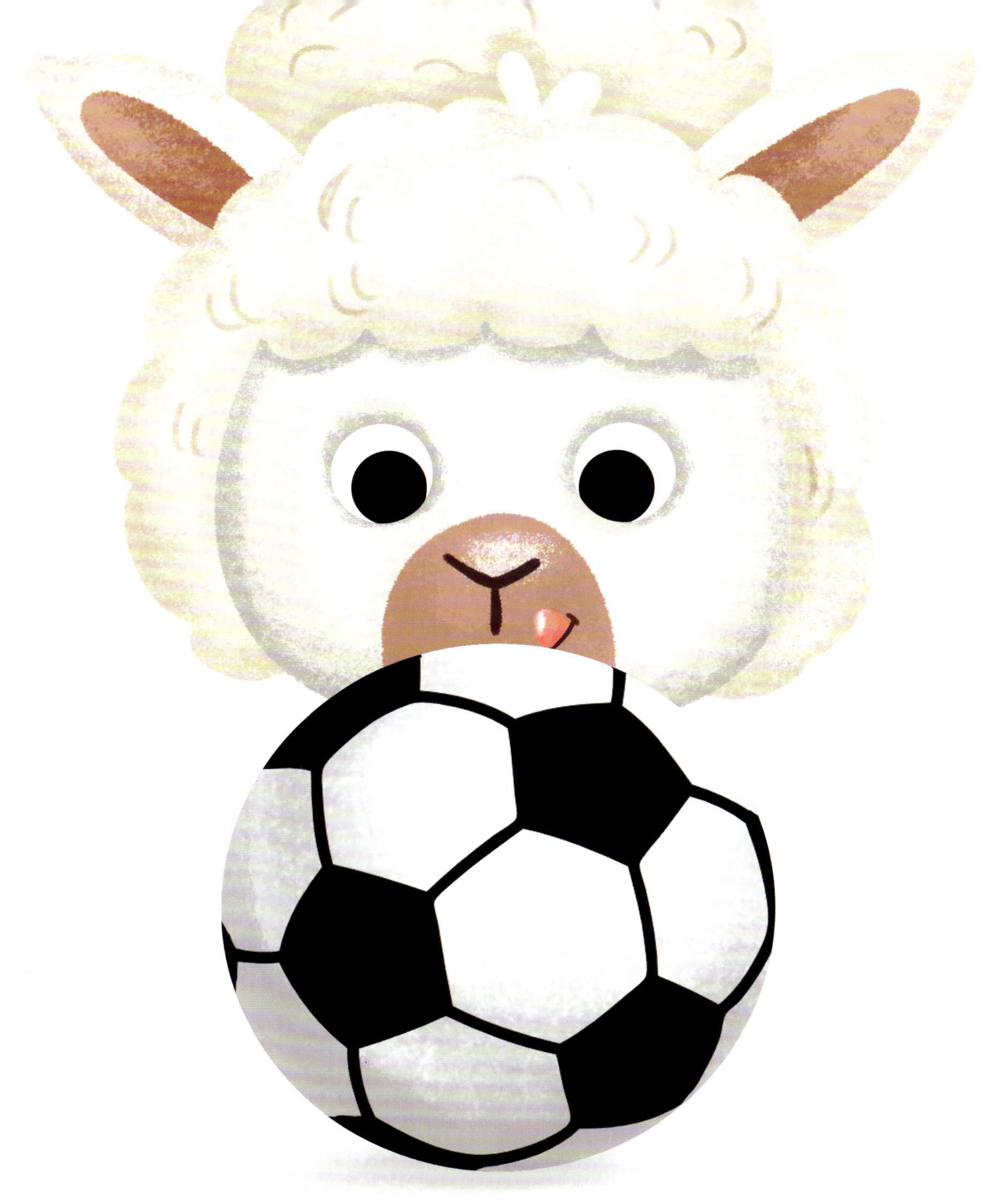

While the tapir talks, one pupil's busy **playing**.
She doesn't listen **carefully** to what her teacher's saying.

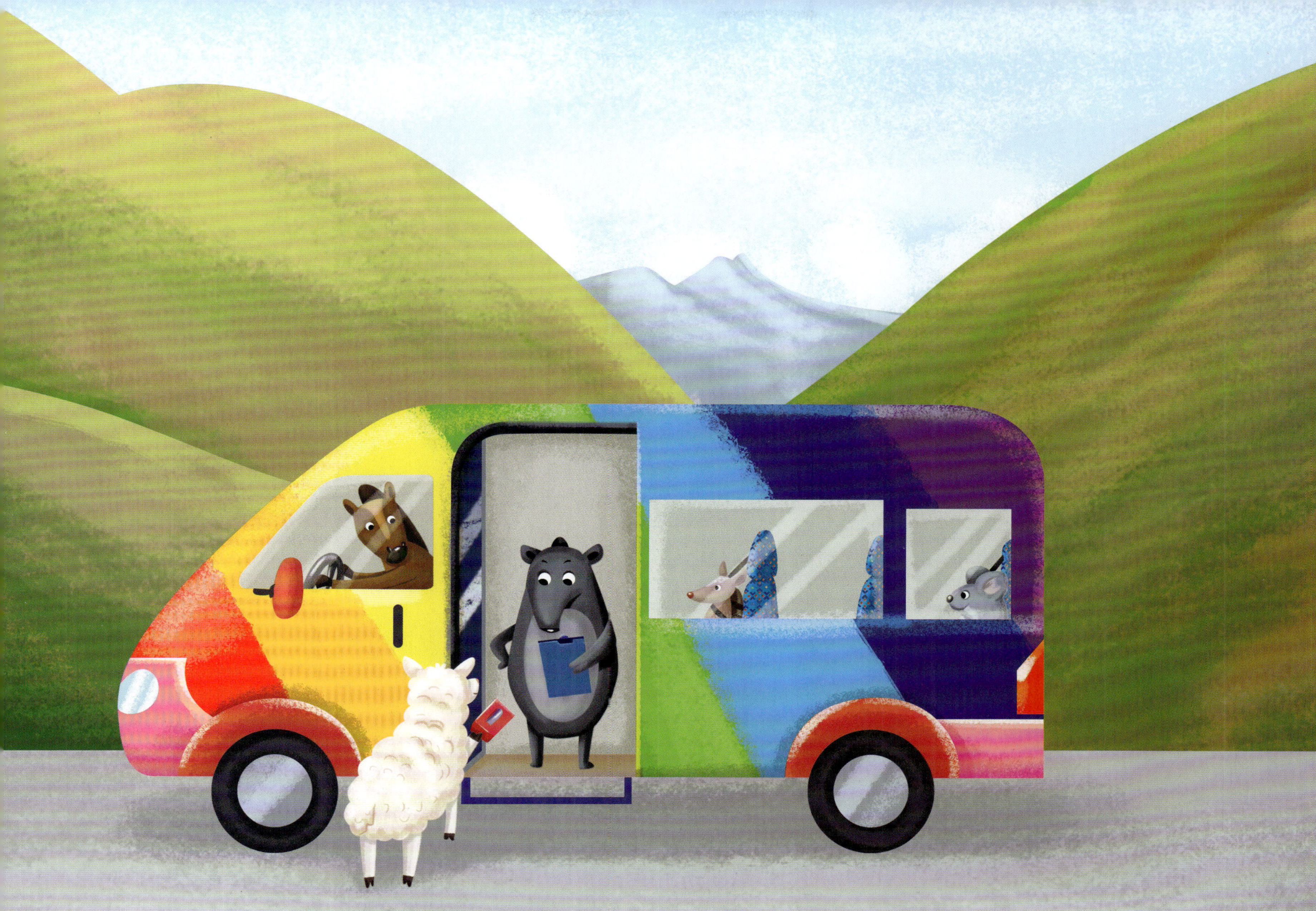

So next day when they all arrive, she doesn't have a **hat**,
she didn't bring a **water bottle** and doesn't have a **snack**.
Llama boards the coach with her lunch box held up high.
"At least I've got my lunch," she shrugs, and teacher gives a **sigh**.

Finally, they're all **aboard**; the teacher checks his list.
He makes sure everyone is there and nobody's been missed.
"Right then!" he announces. "We'll soon be on our way.
Can anyone remember what we're going to see today?"

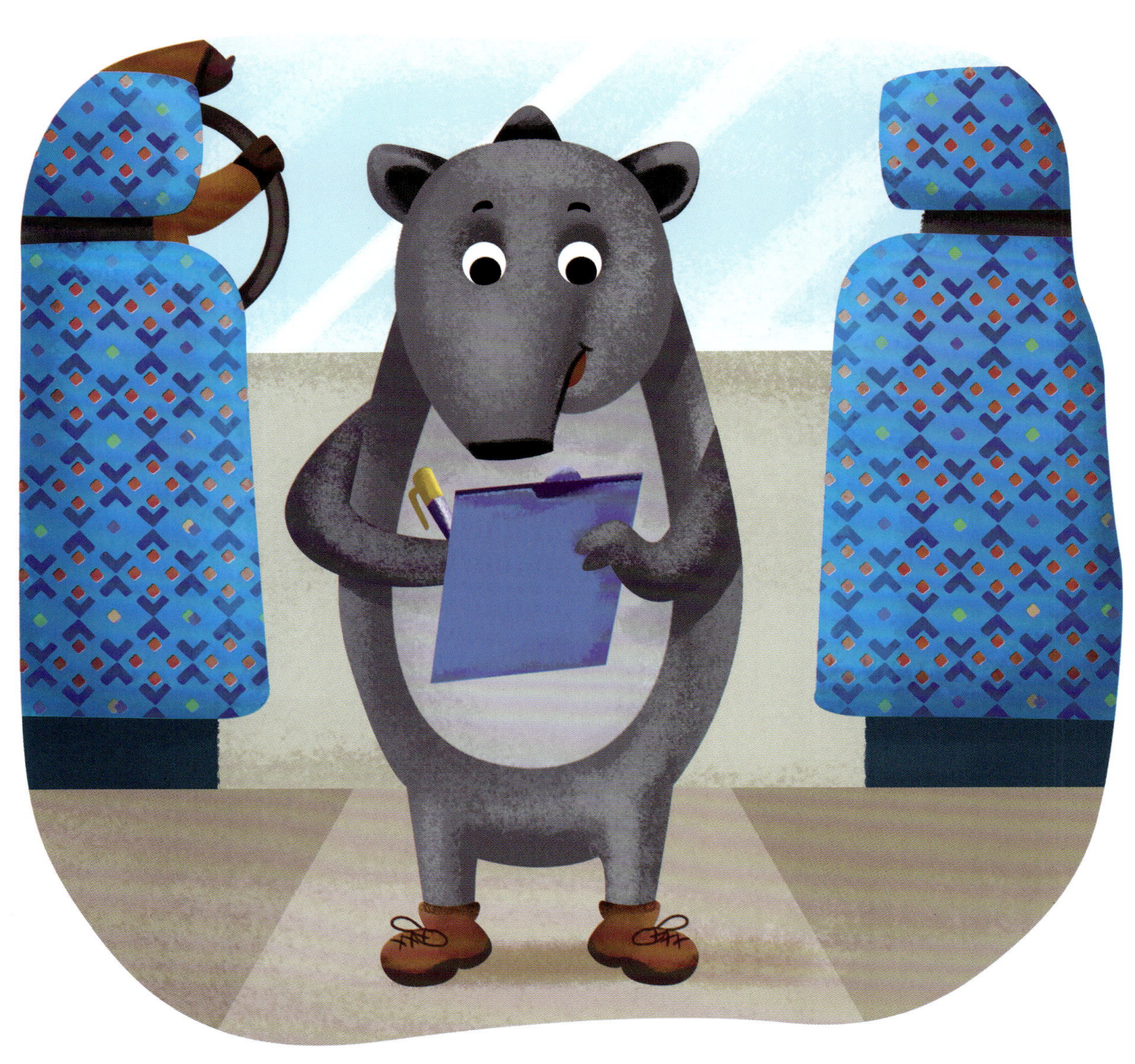

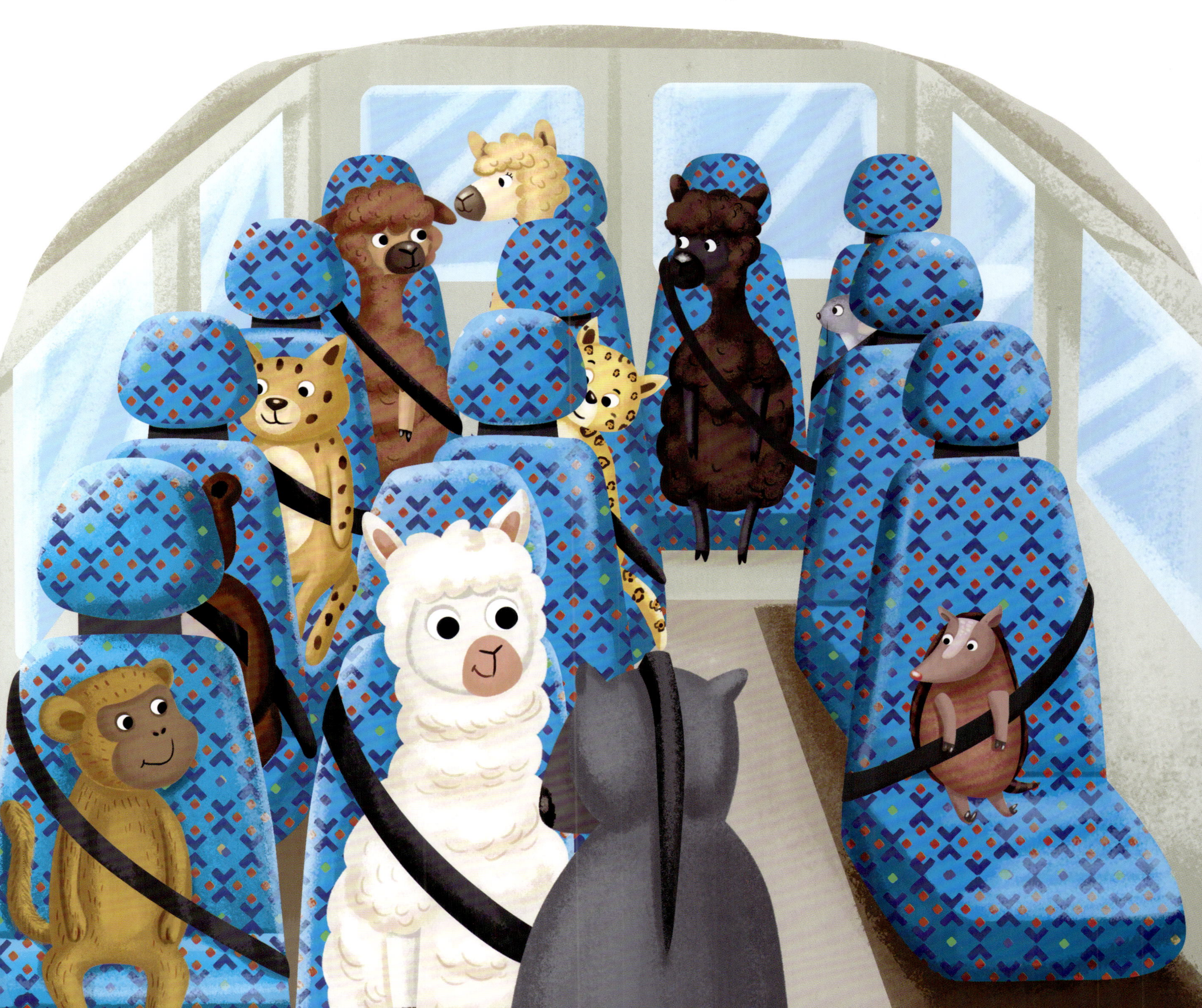

"No, it's not a **waterfall**… No, it's not a **fountain**…
We are setting off to see the famous **Rainbow Mountain!**"

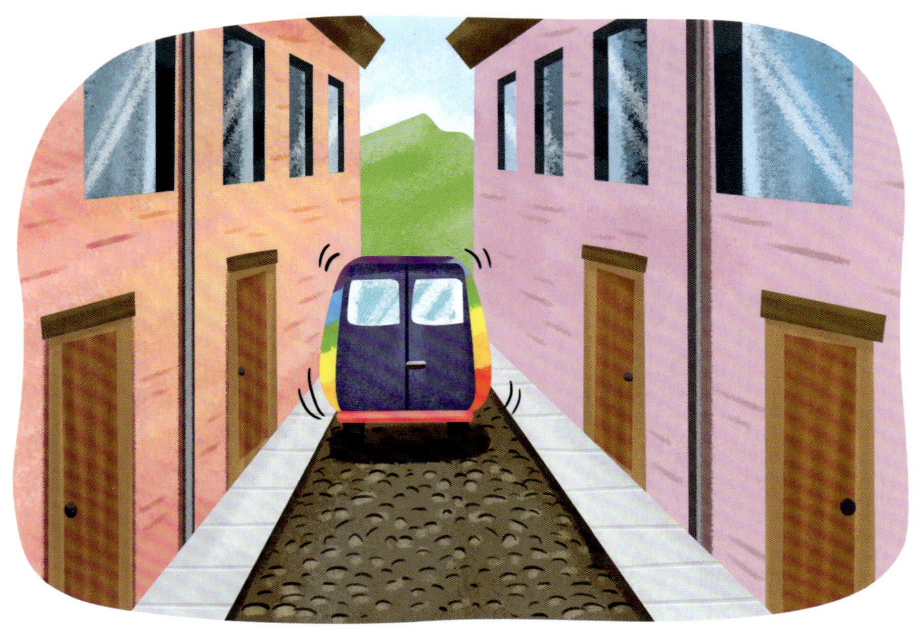

They **rumble** down the road and **squeeze** along an alley.

They **climb** the most enormous hill...

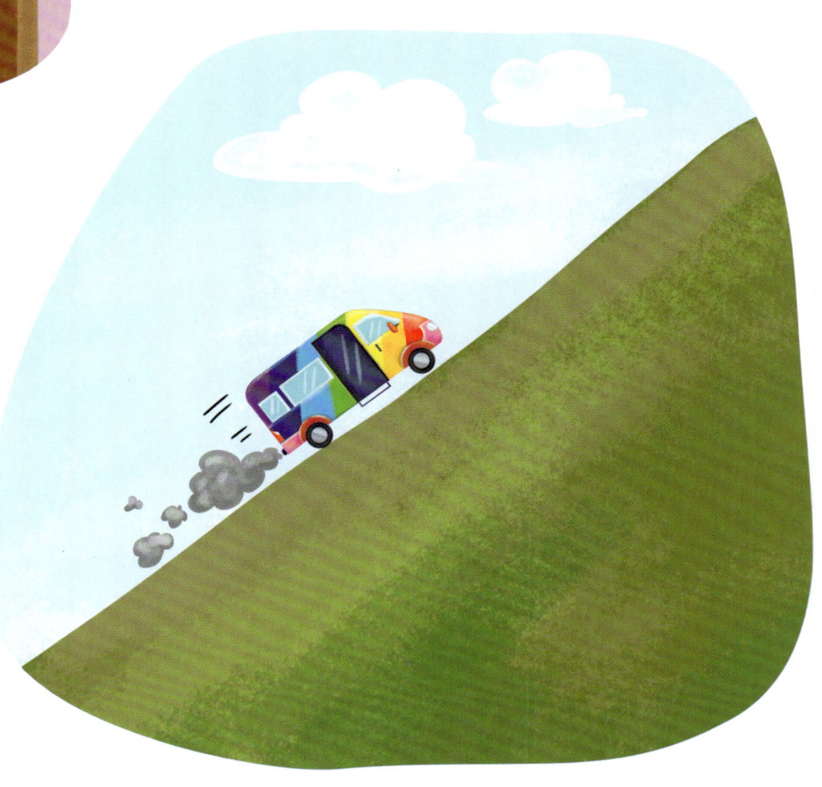

...and **chug** along the valley.

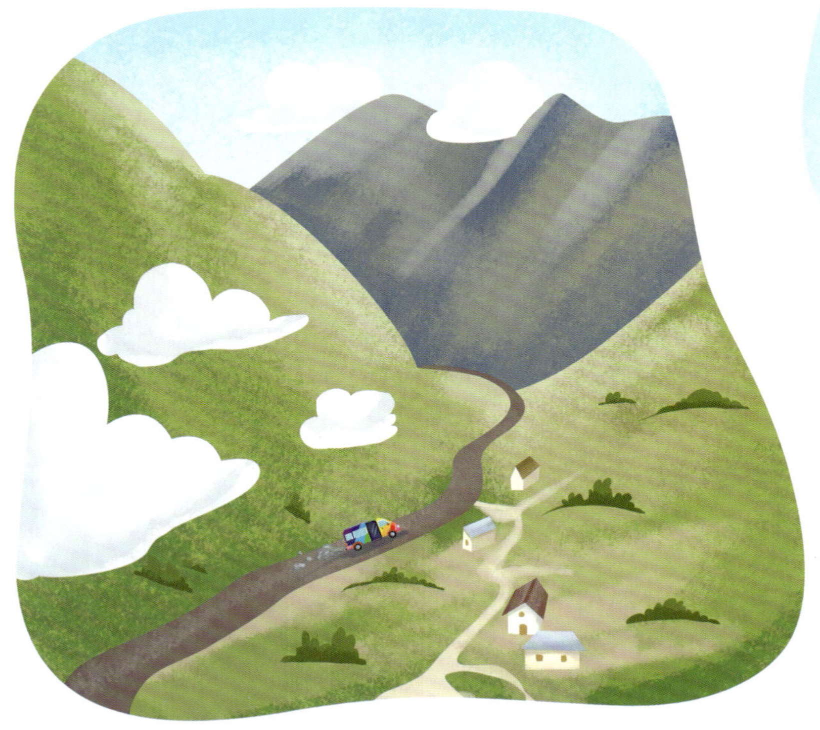

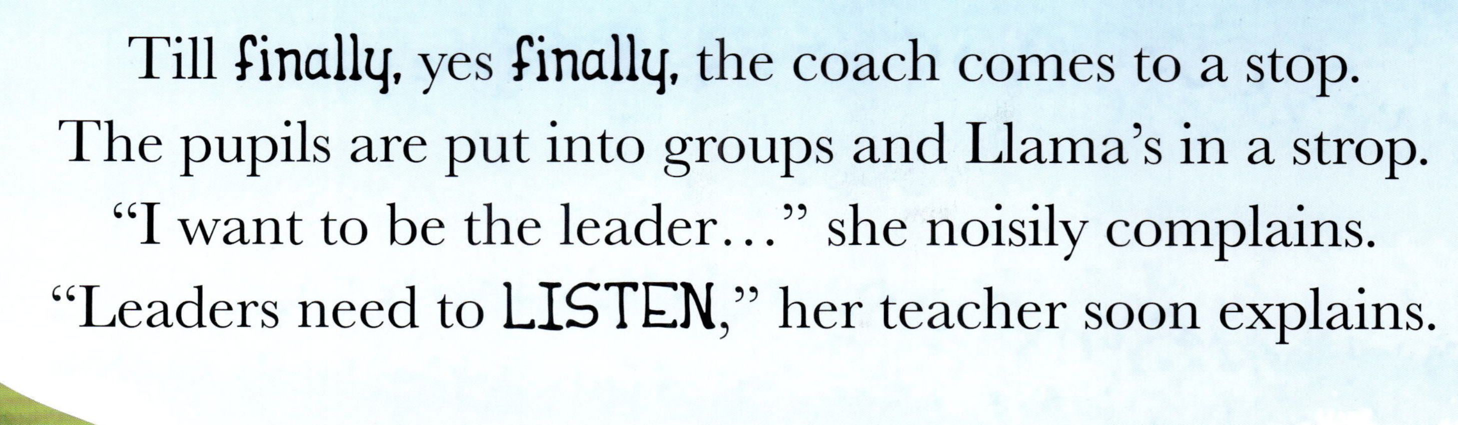

Till **finally**, yes **finally**, the coach comes to a stop.
The pupils are put into groups and Llama's in a strop.
"I want to be the leader…" she noisily complains.
"Leaders need to LISTEN," her teacher soon explains.

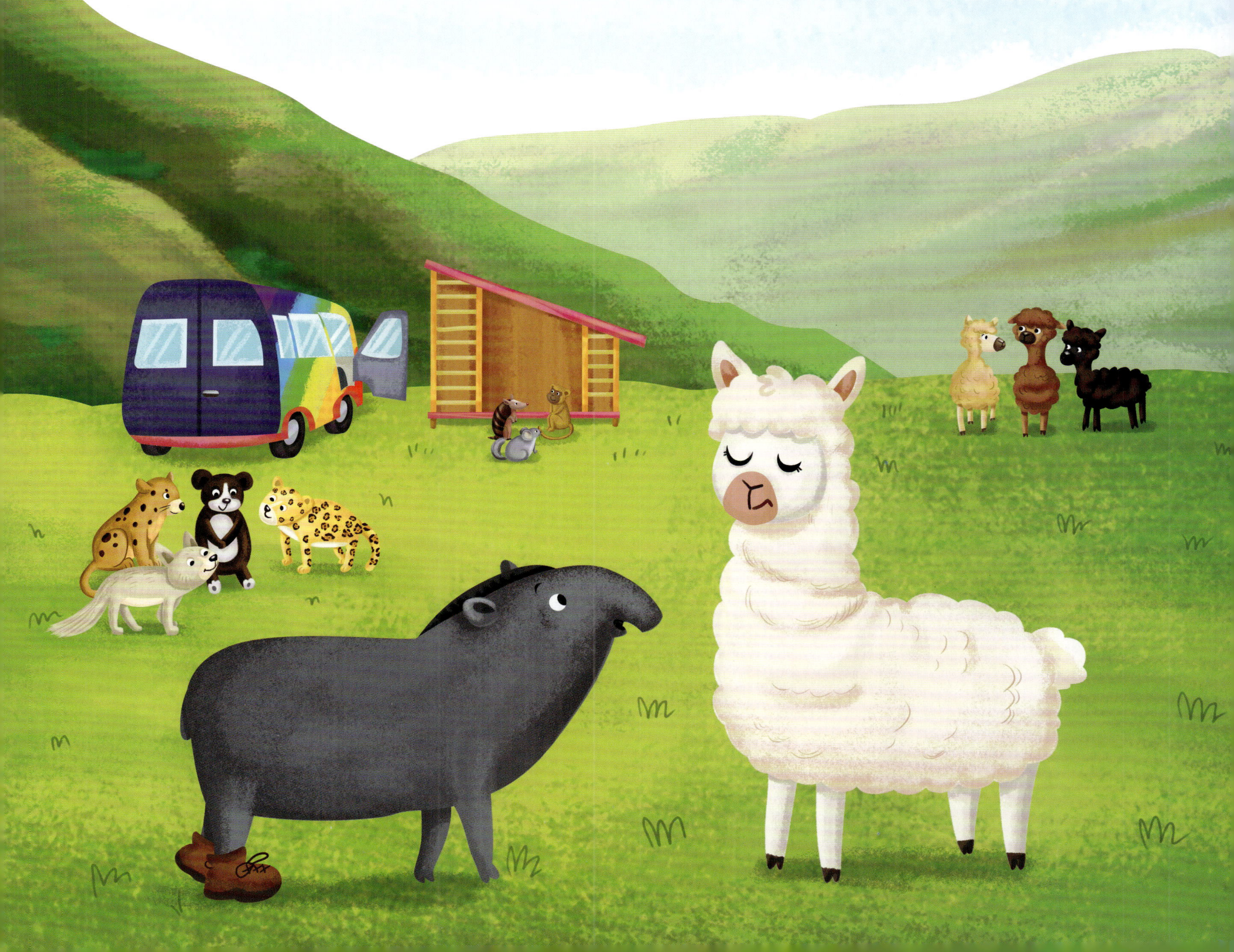

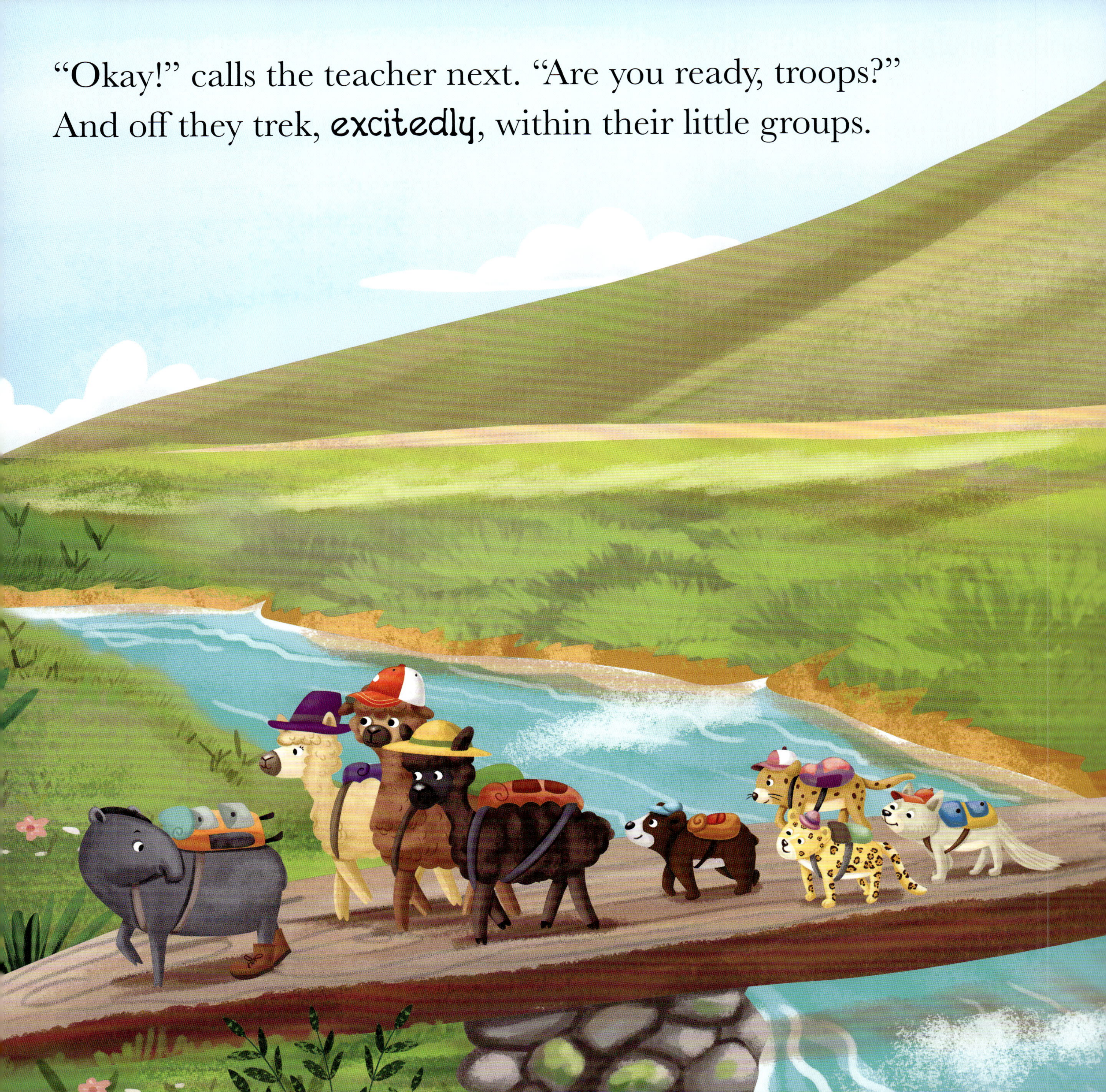
"Okay!" calls the teacher next. "Are you ready, troops?"
And off they trek, excitedly, within their little groups.

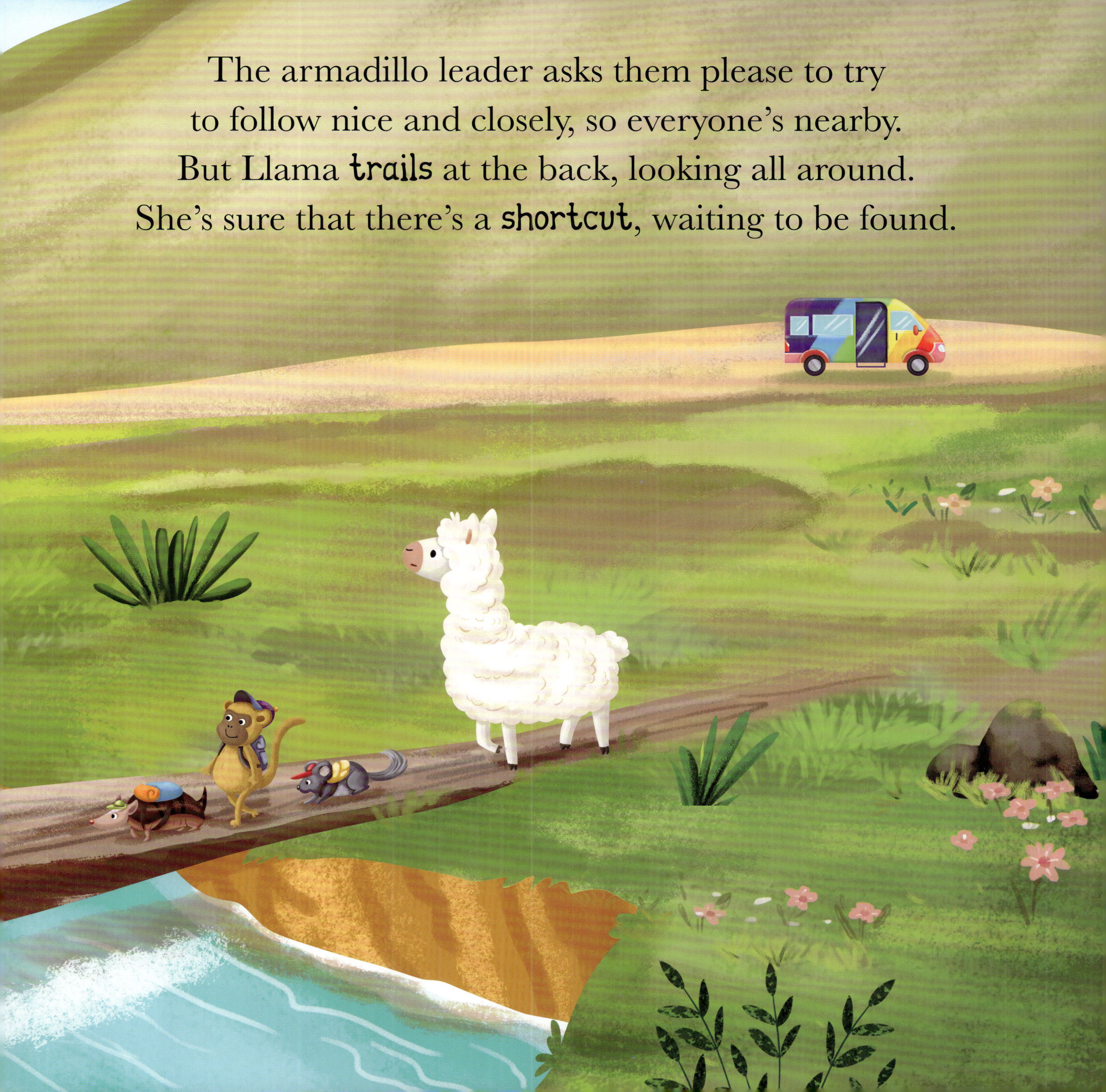

The armadillo leader asks them please to try
to follow nice and closely, so everyone's nearby.
But Llama **trails** at the back, looking all around.
She's sure that there's a **shortcut**, waiting to be found.

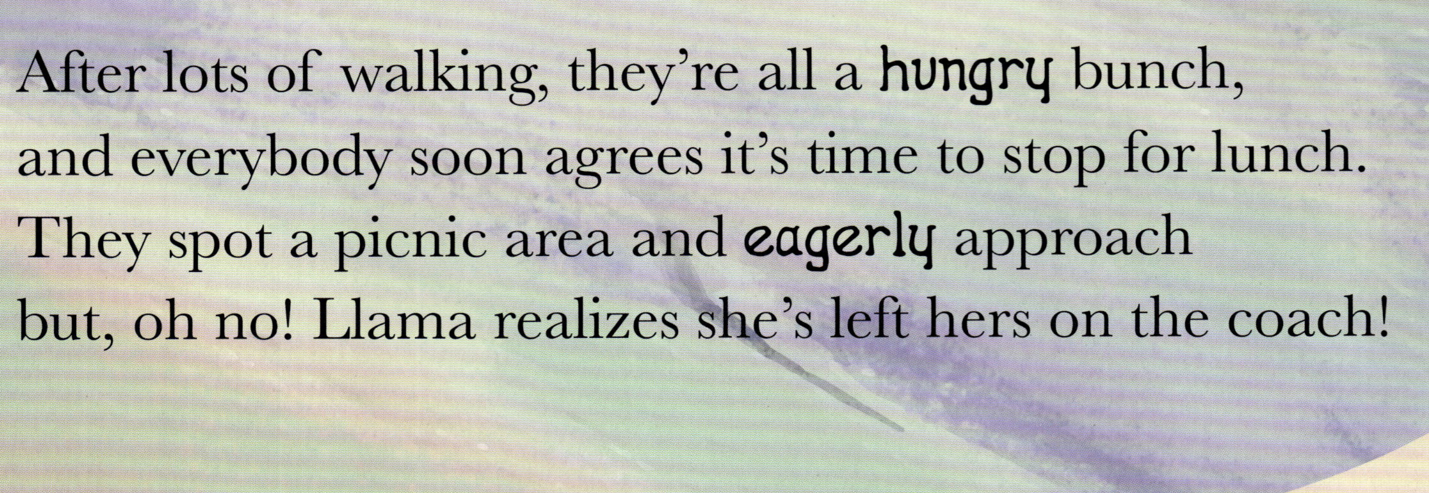

After lots of walking, they're all a **hungry** bunch,
and everybody soon agrees it's time to stop for lunch.
They spot a picnic area and **eagerly** approach
but, oh no! Llama realizes she's left hers on the coach!

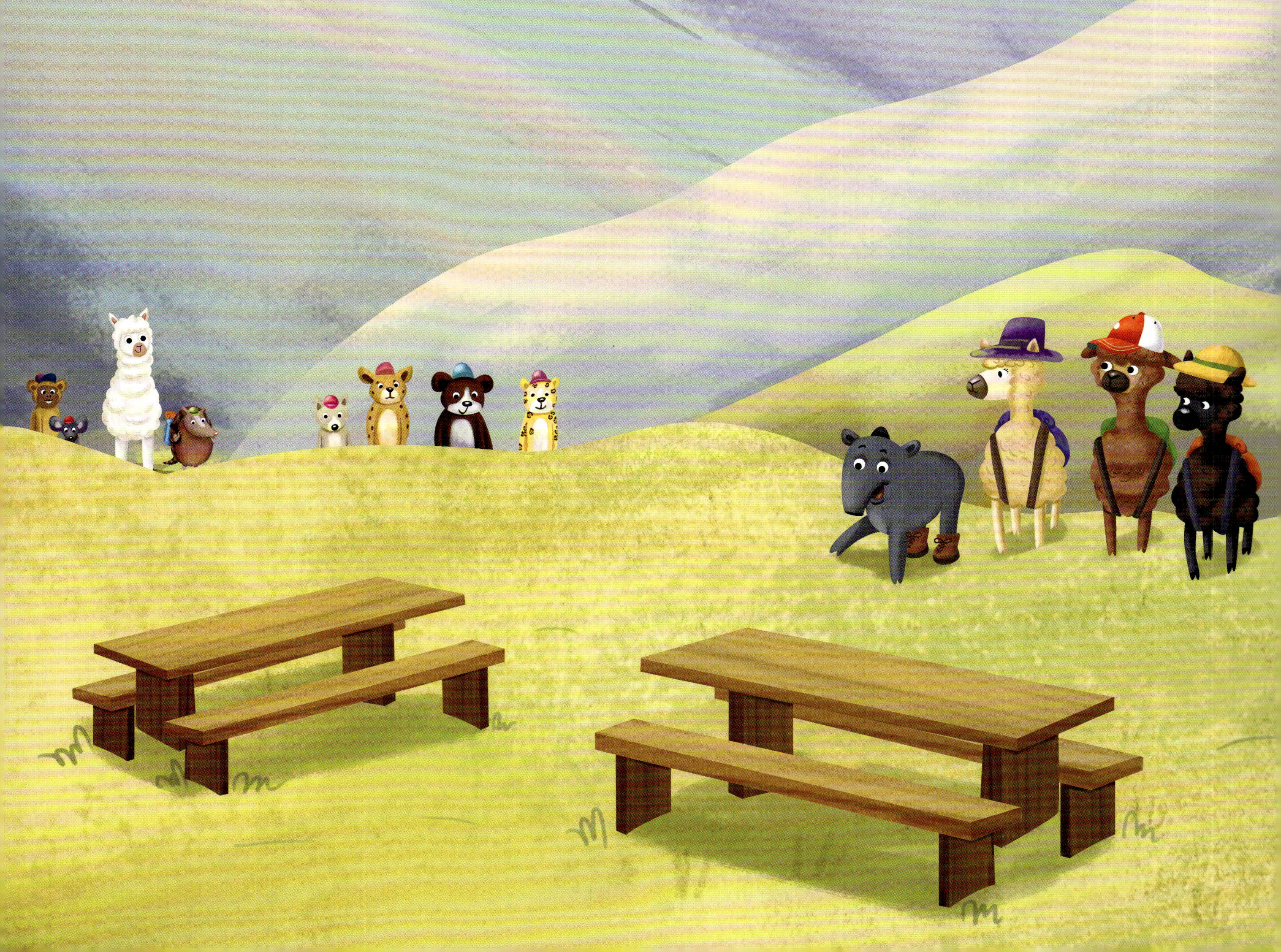

"Llama never listens…" her classmates softly **mumble**.
Reluctantly, they share their food, trying not to **grumble**.

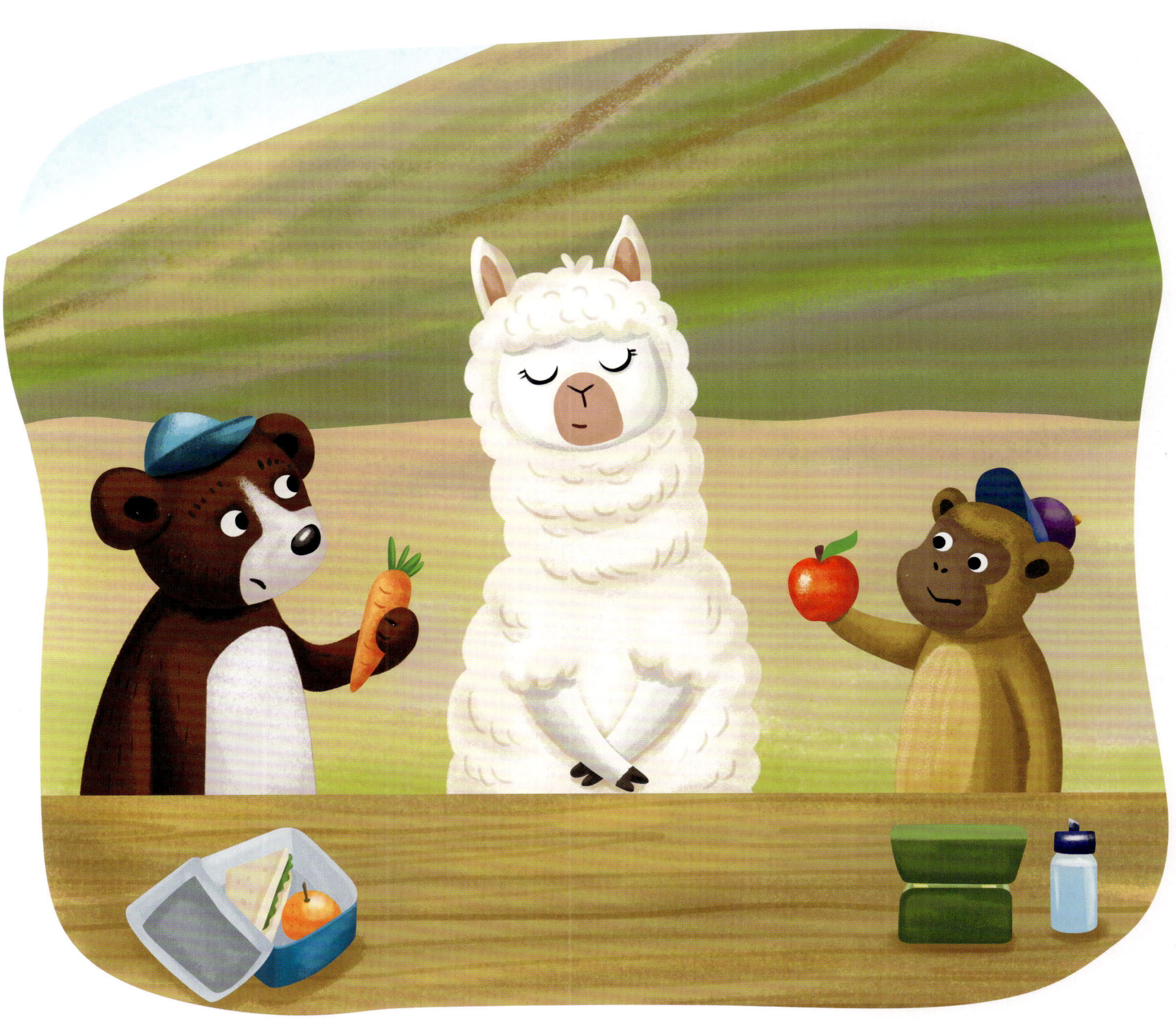

After lunch, the tapir scans his map to check the route.
He shows them all while Llama munches **loudly** on some fruit.
Before long, they have all packed up and everyone is **walking**.
"Be careful!" Armadillo calls but Llama's busy **talking**.

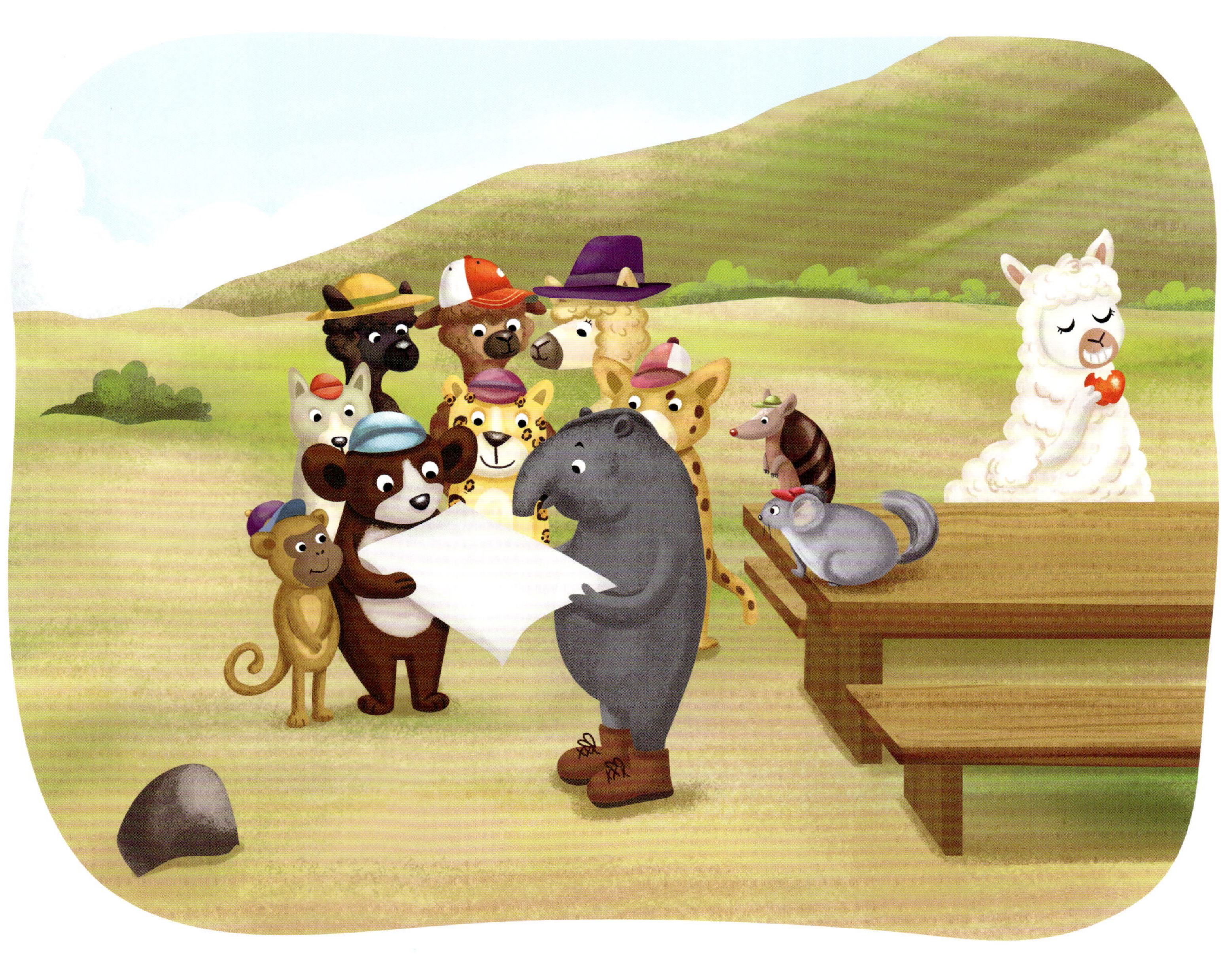

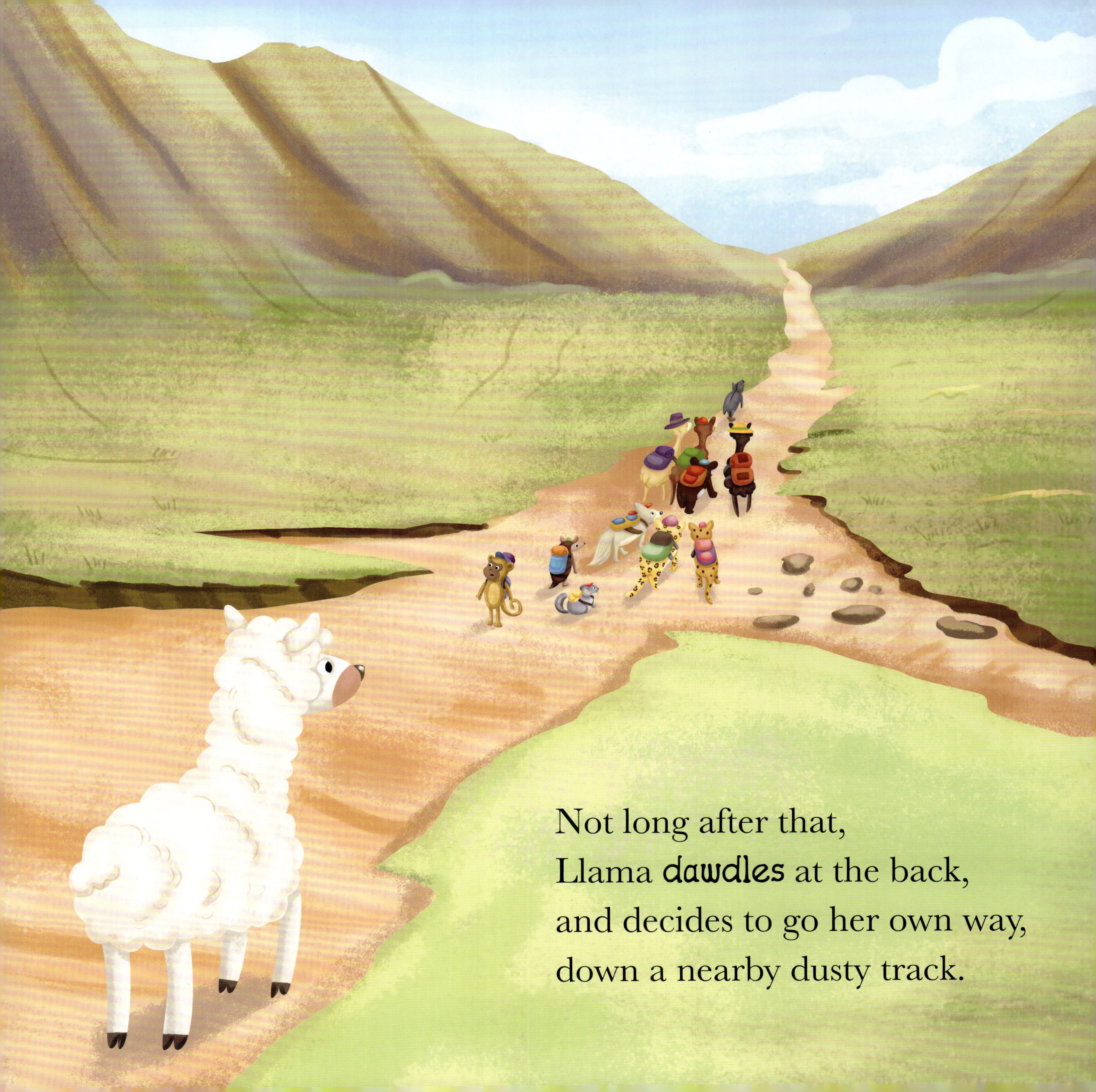

Not long after that,
Llama **dawdles** at the back,
and decides to go her own way,
down a nearby dusty track.

Llama's trotting happily along the **stony** ground,
totally convinced that she's Rainbow-Mountain-bound,
when the **bumpy** path gets narrower and then just...

...**disappears!**

She turns to find a crossroads
and her eyes **fill** with hot tears.

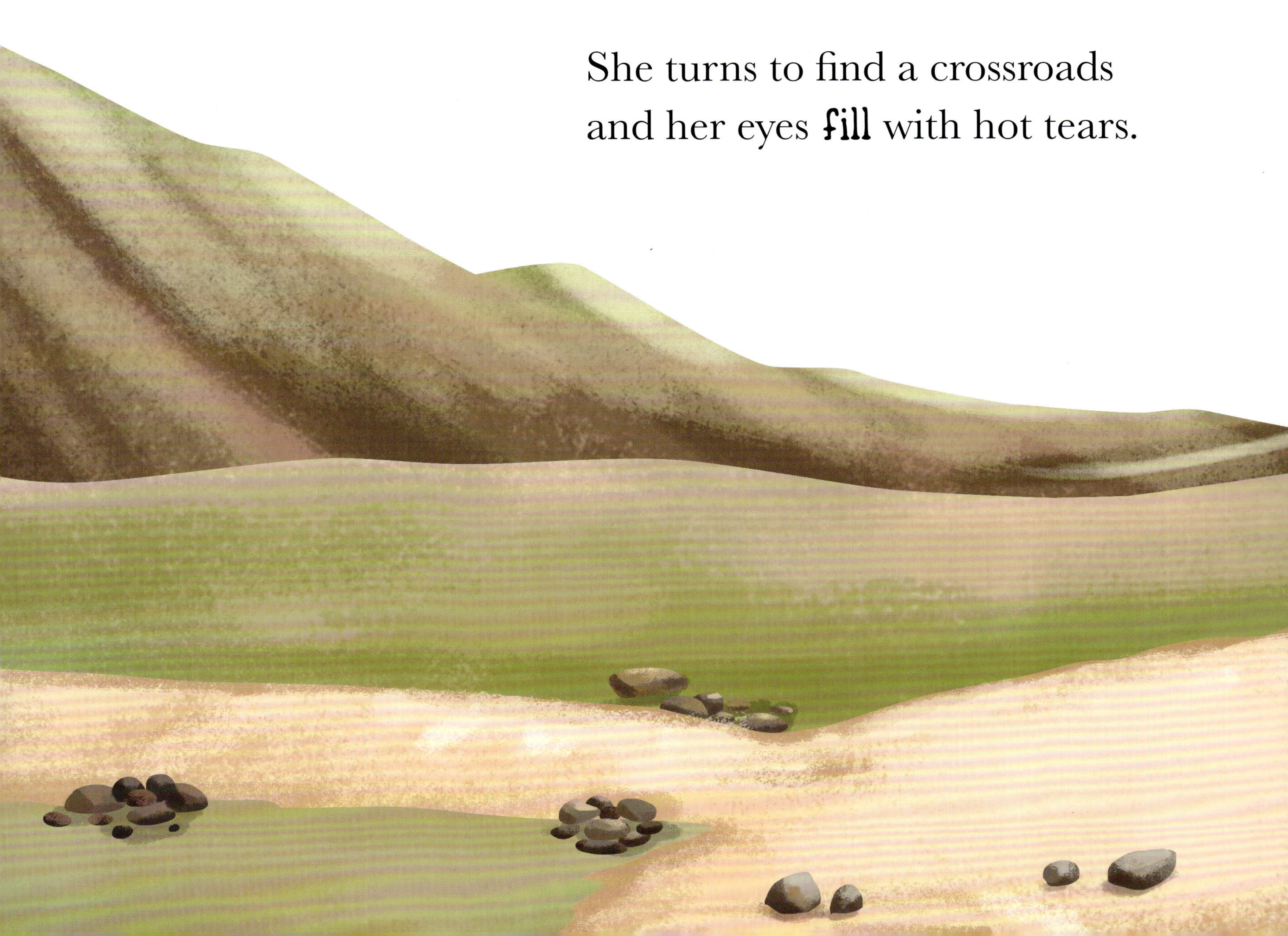

She **tries** to conjure up a memory of the teacher's map.
Oh, why wasn't she listening?! She can't find her way back!

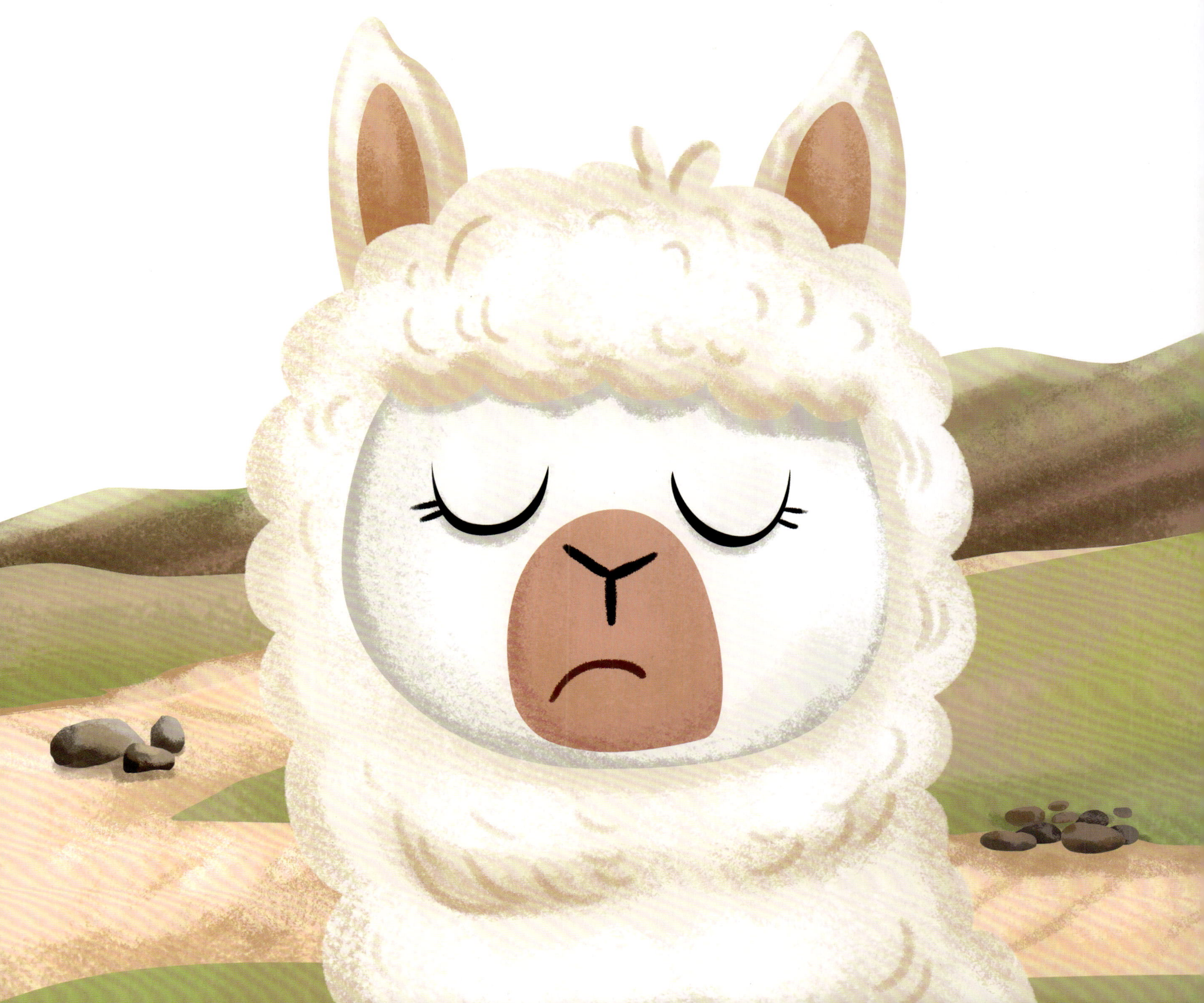

Meanwhile, Armadillo spots that someone's gone **astray**.

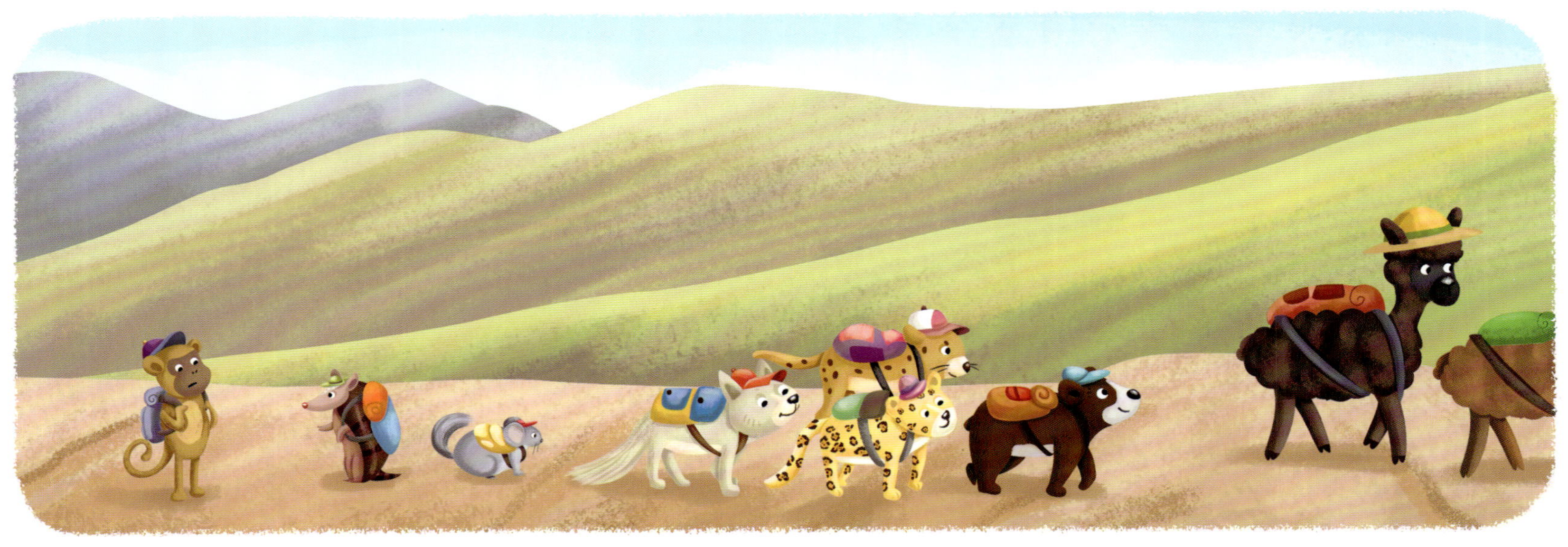

"It's Llama," mumbles Monkey. "She went a different way..."

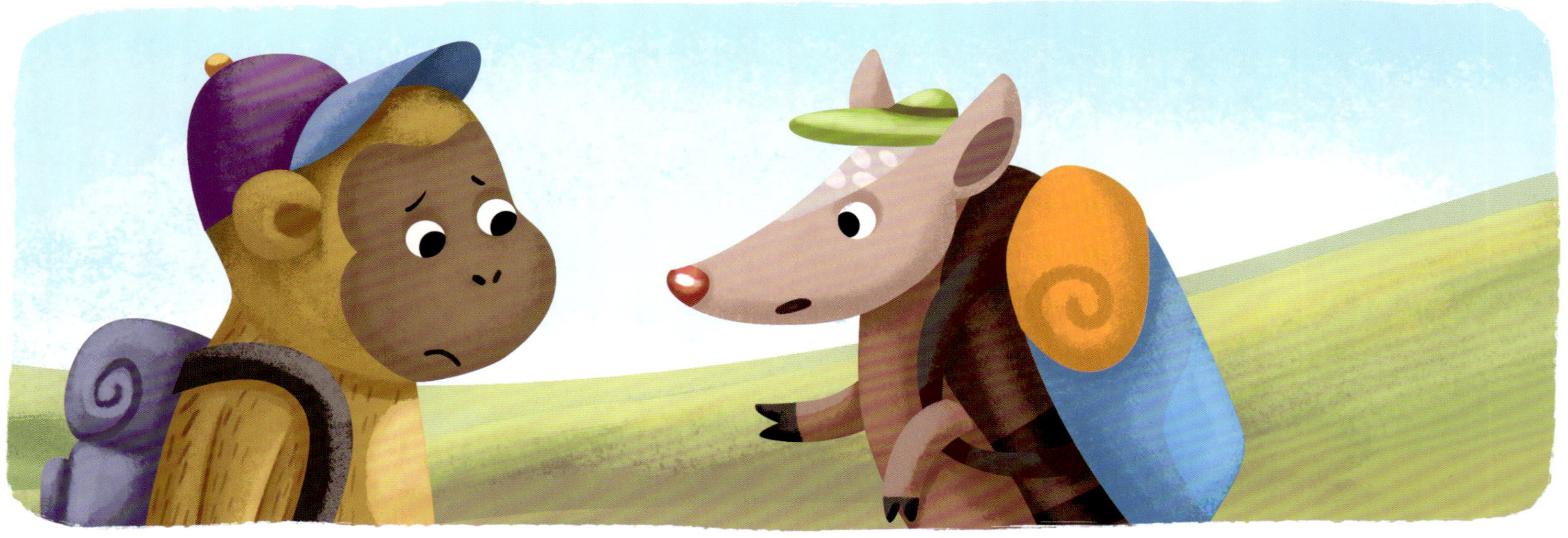

Armadillo sighs, and their teacher is quite **cross**.
"I'd better go and find her. She's probably got **lost**.
You guys carry on – you're very nearly there.
We'll try to catch you up…" His eyes roll in **despair**.

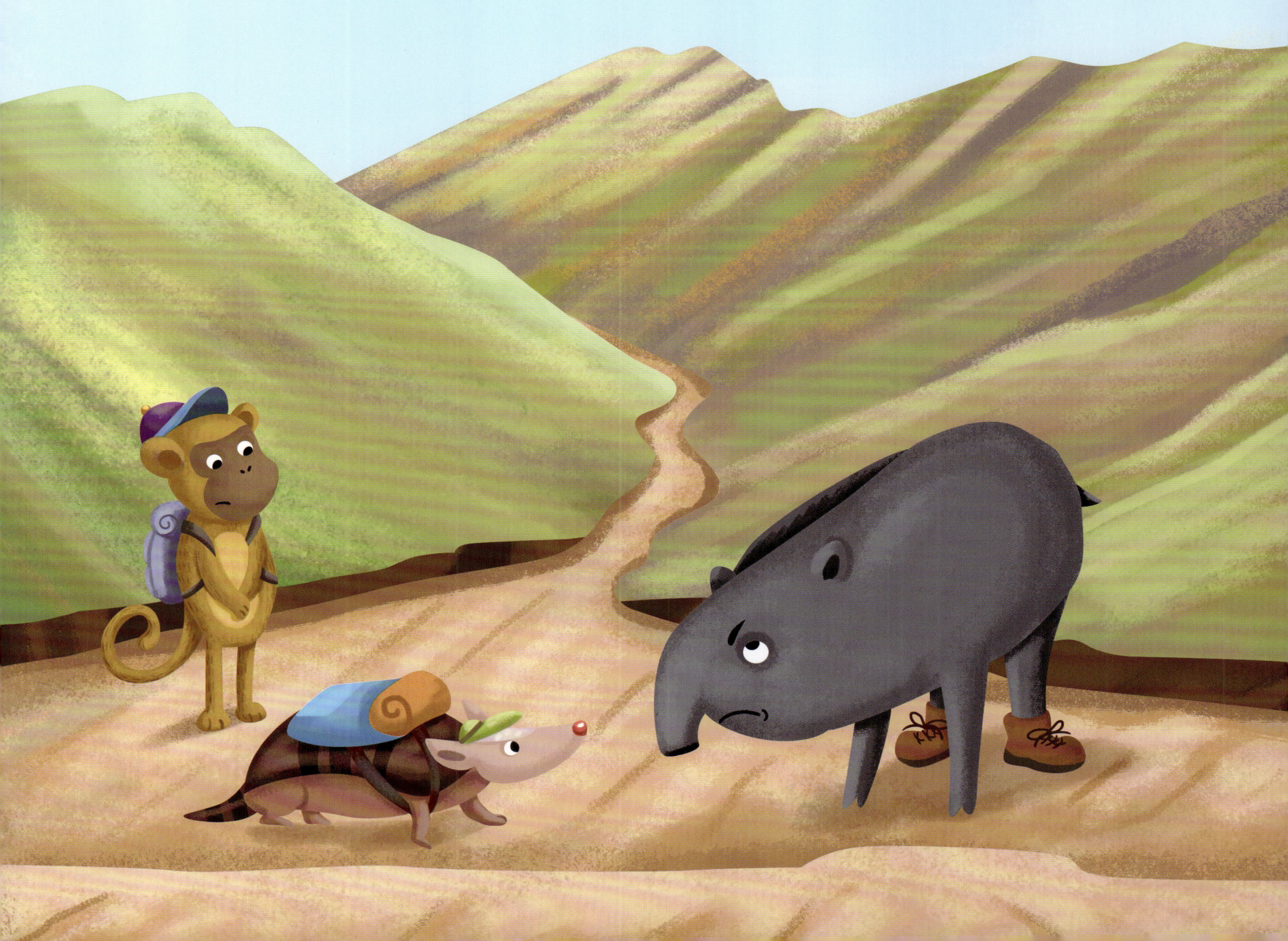

The teacher hasn't
gone far when he spots
some **pointy** ears.

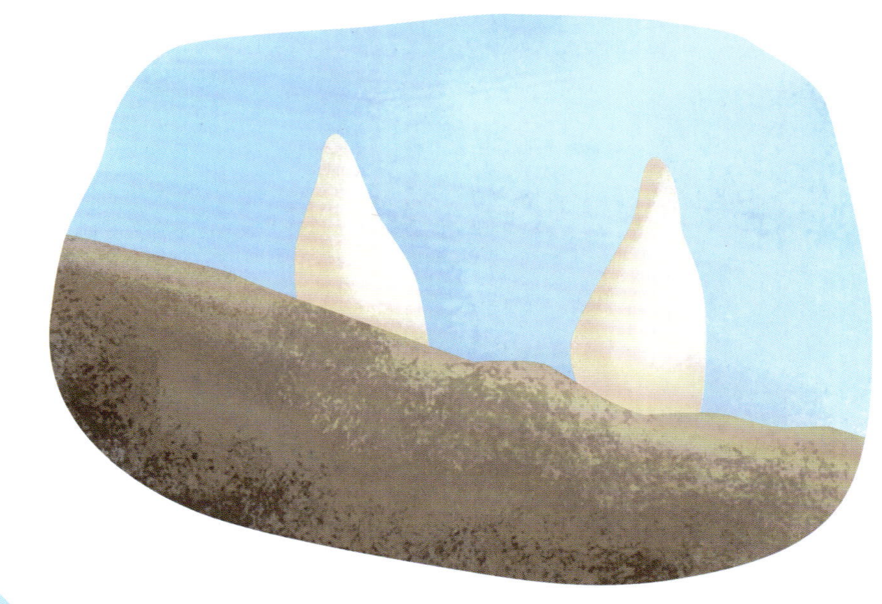

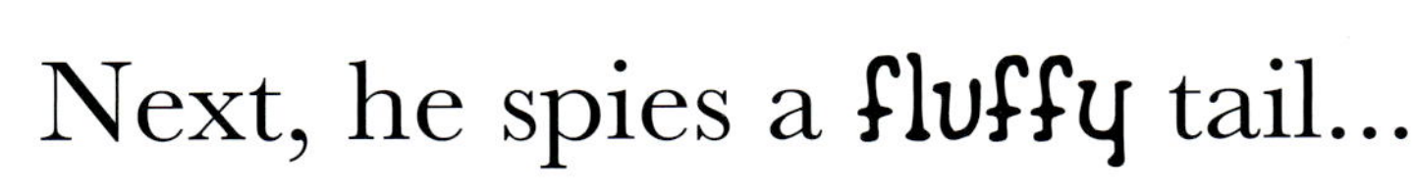

Next, he spies a **fluffy** tail...

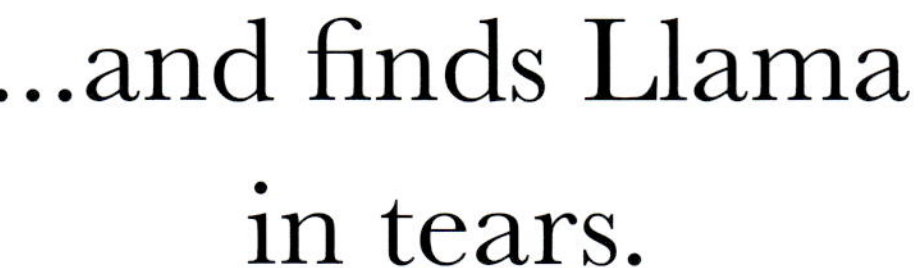

...and finds Llama
in tears.

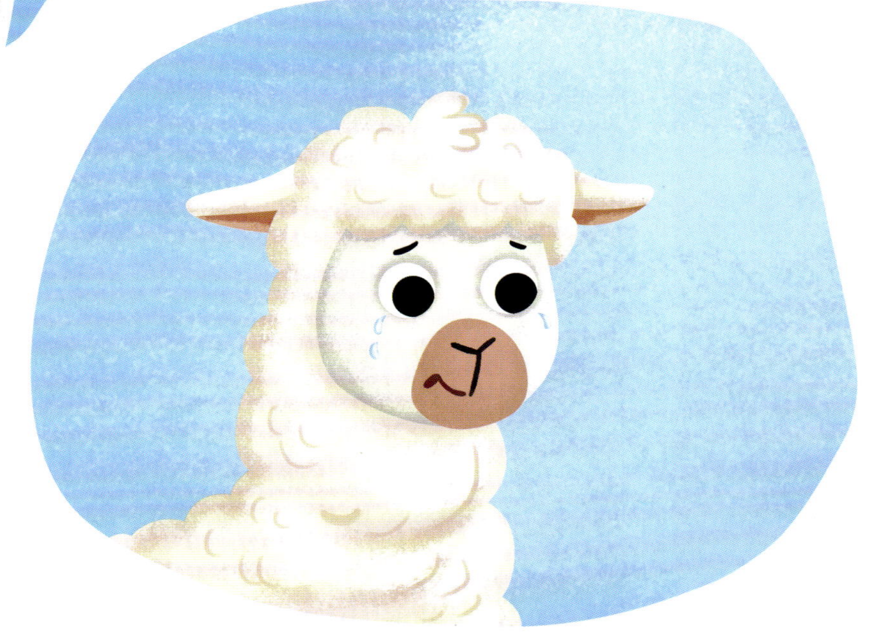

"Don't worry," says the tapir. "I'm here now – you're alright.
You shouldn't have gone off like that. You gave us all a **fright**.
Perhaps you'll **listen** next time?" And Llama nods her head.
"Let's go and find your classmates. They're not too far ahead."

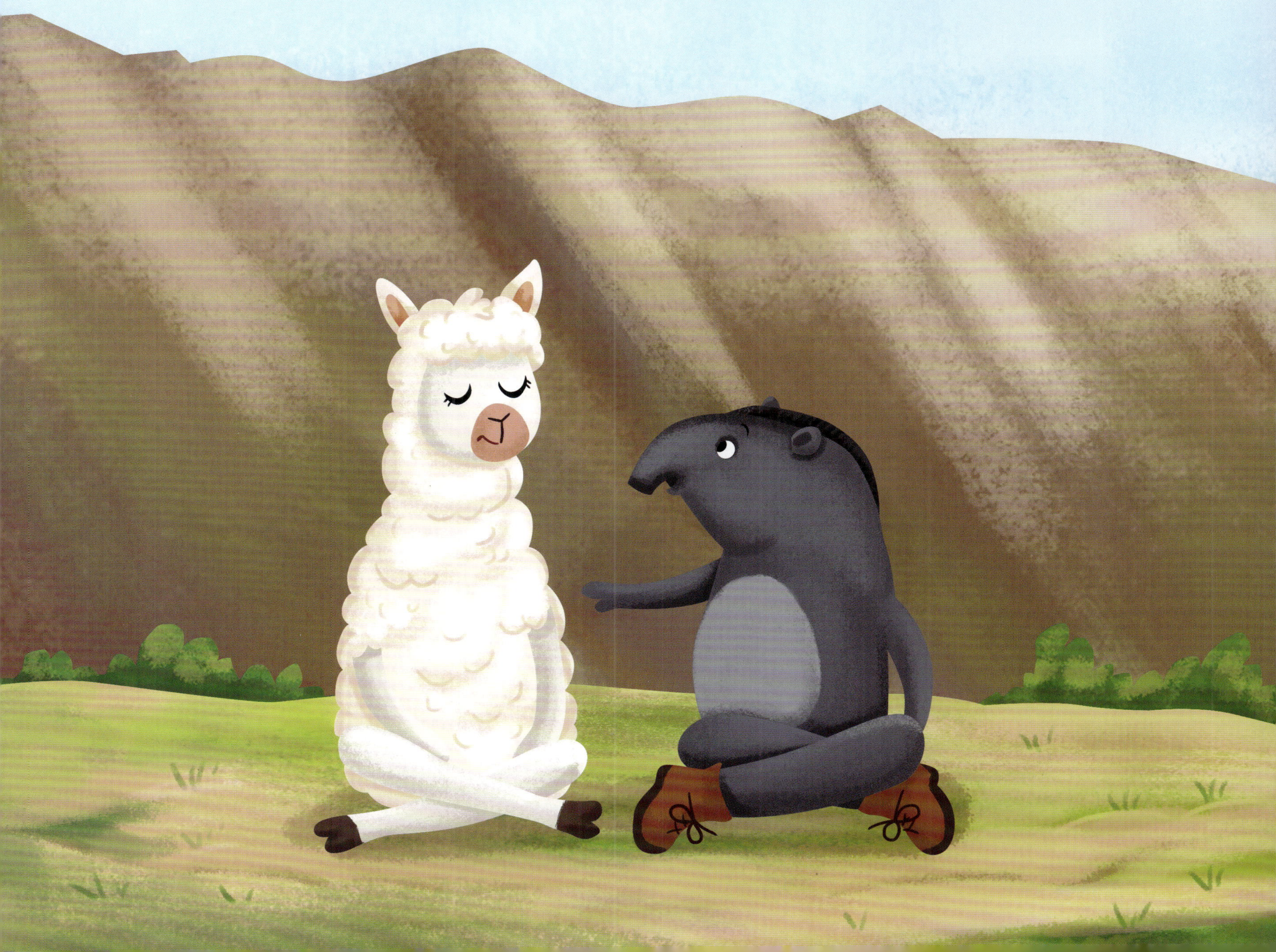

The pair draw near and find the others **silently** just gazing.
"Wow," says Llama quietly. It really is **amazing**…
The mountain's **gold** and **crimson**, **purple**, **pink** and **green**.
Llama says, "I think it's the best thing I've EVER seen!"

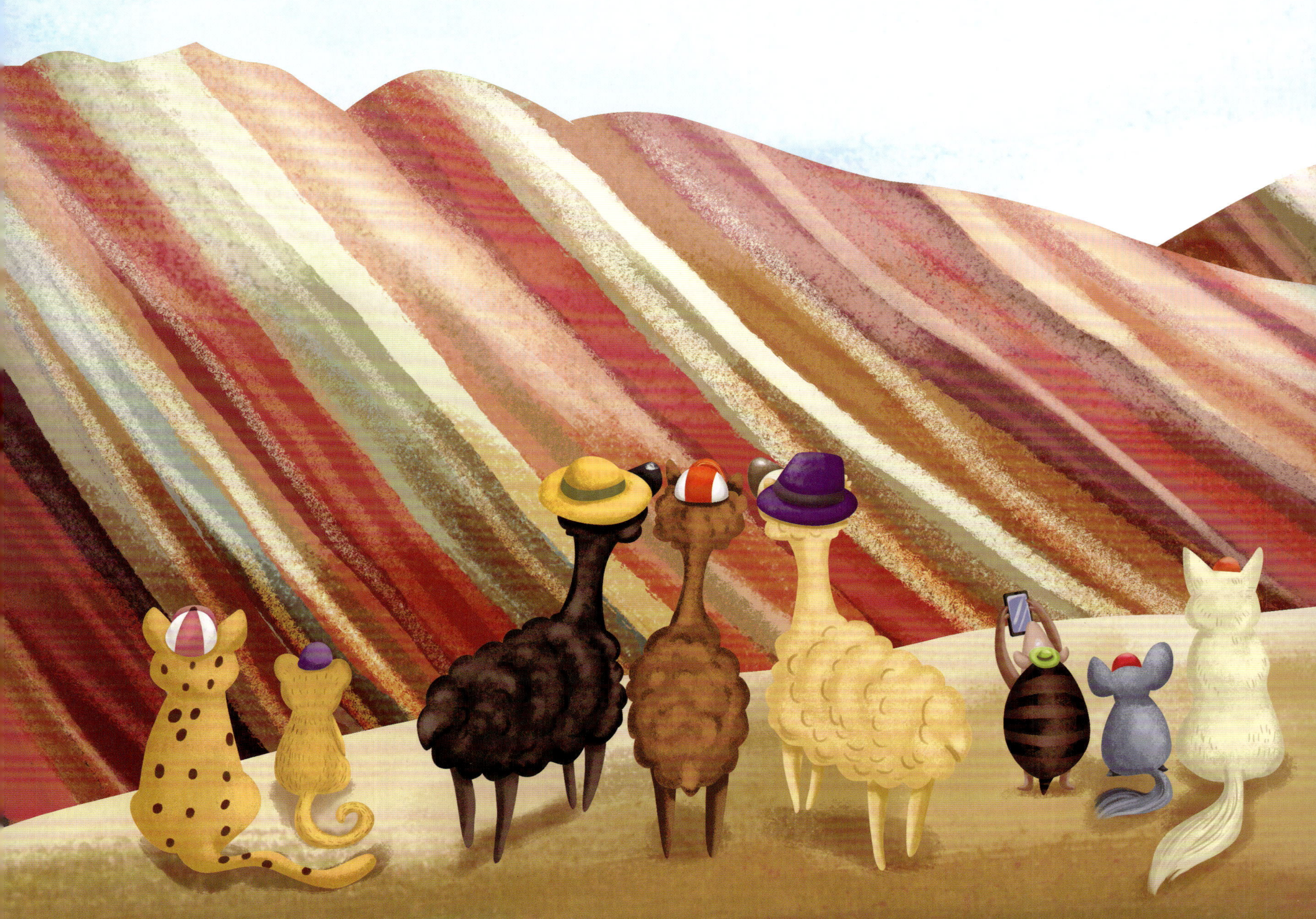

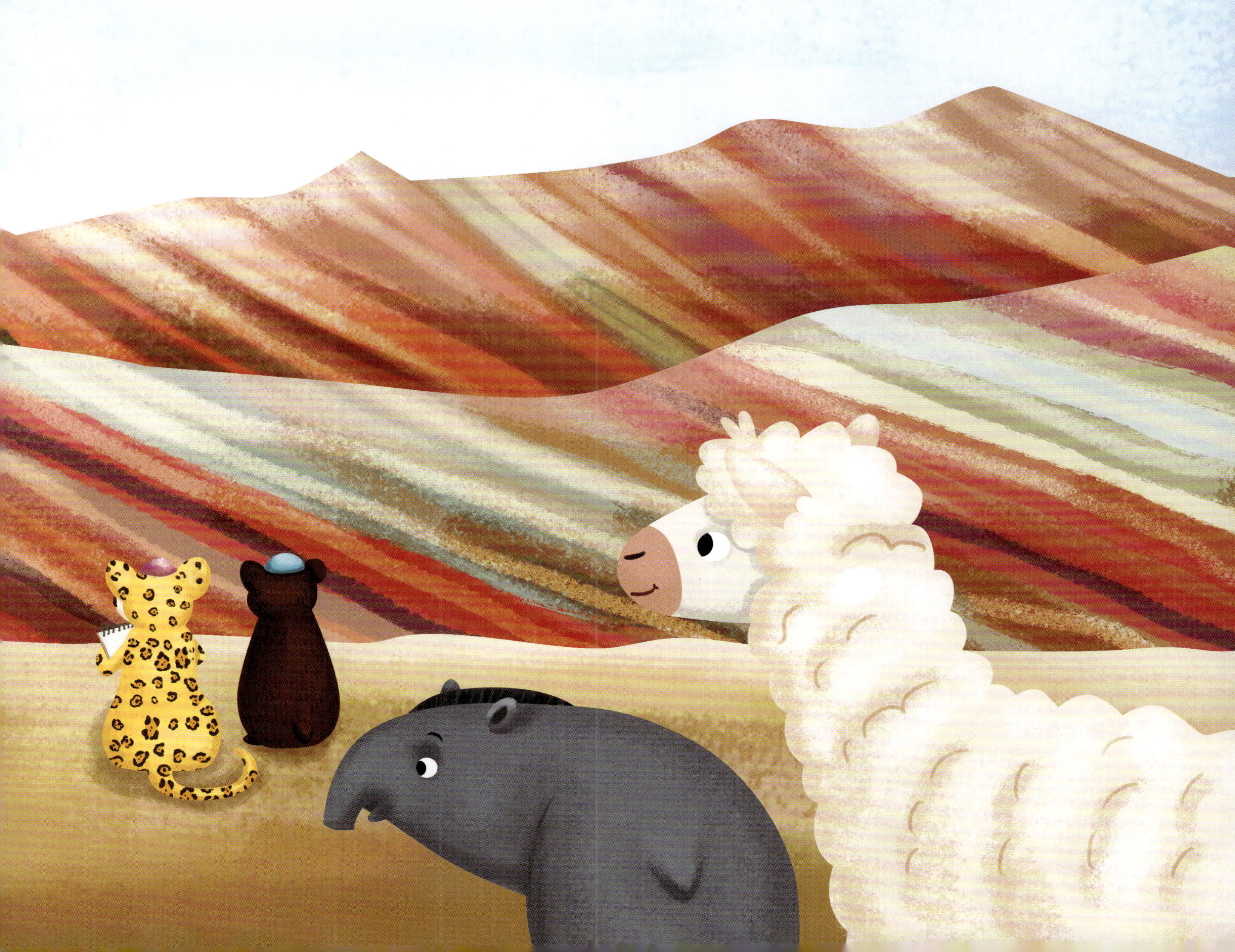

Astounded, some take photos, while others sit and draw until it's time to find the coach and travel back to school.

On the way back home, Llama sits and has a **ponder**.
How sad she'd feel right now if – because of her lone wander –
she hadn't seen the mountain in all its **rainbow glory**.
If someone hadn't found her, it might be a different story.

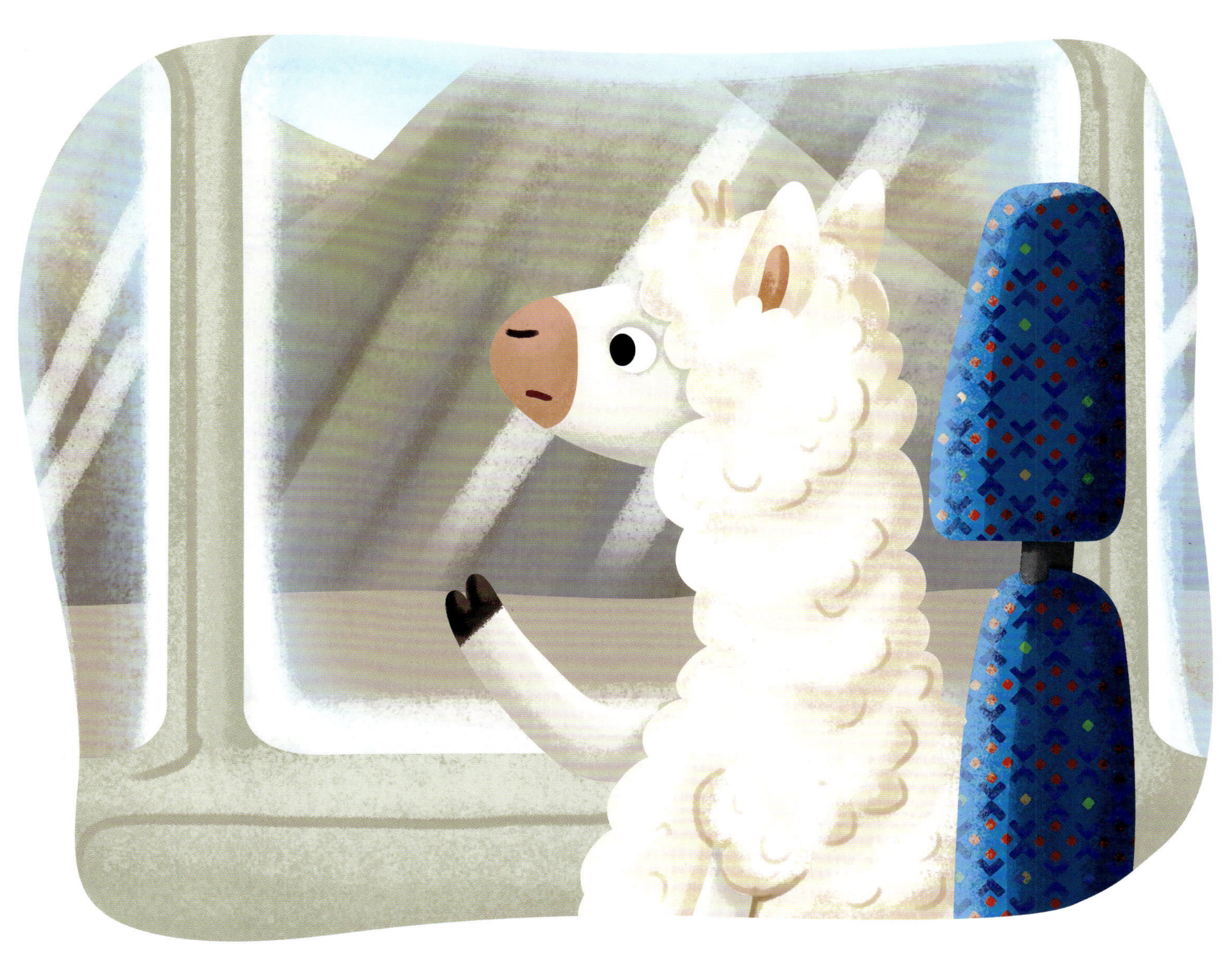

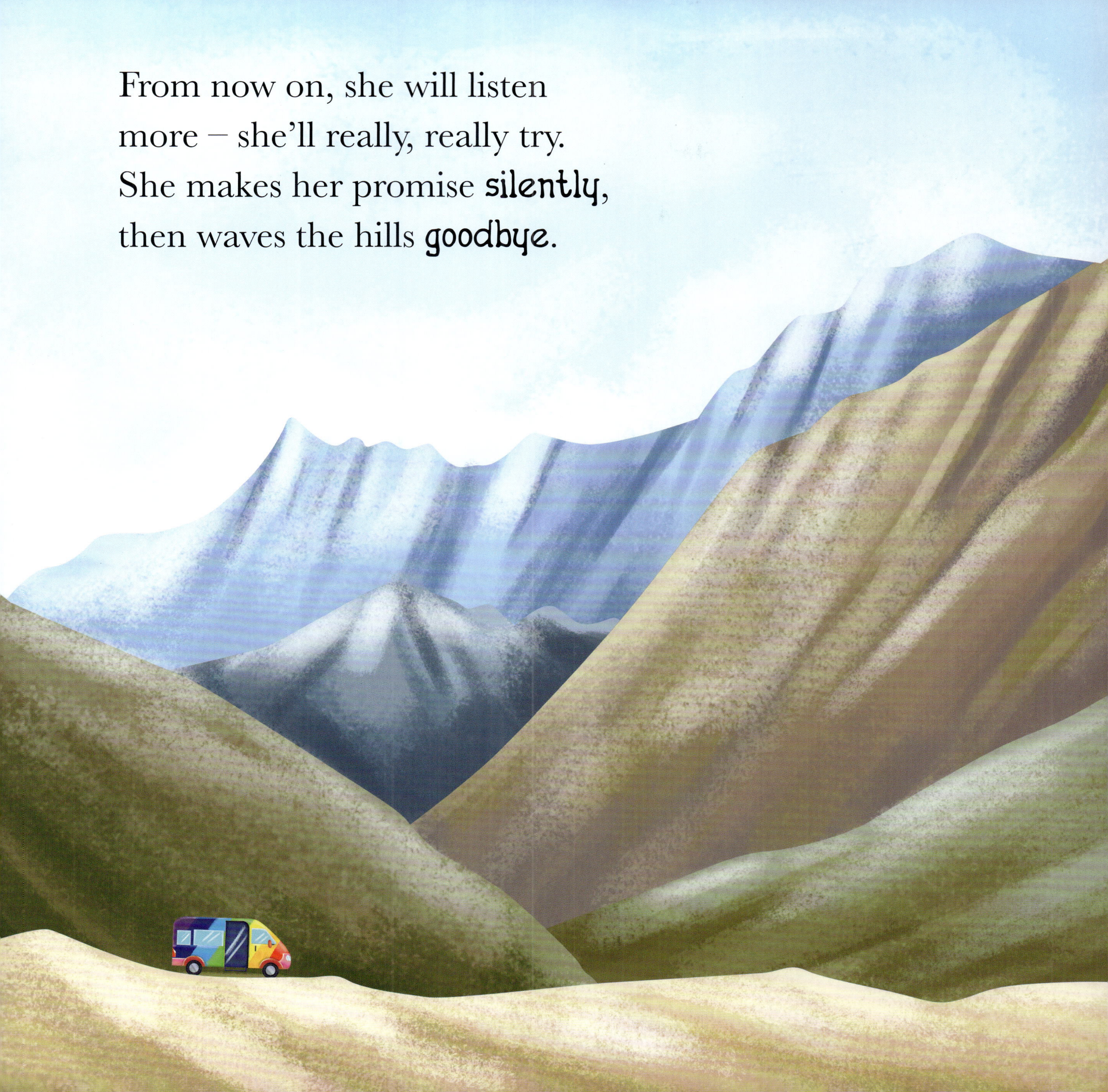

From now on, she will listen
more – she'll really, really try.
She makes her promise **silently**,
then waves the hills **goodbye**.

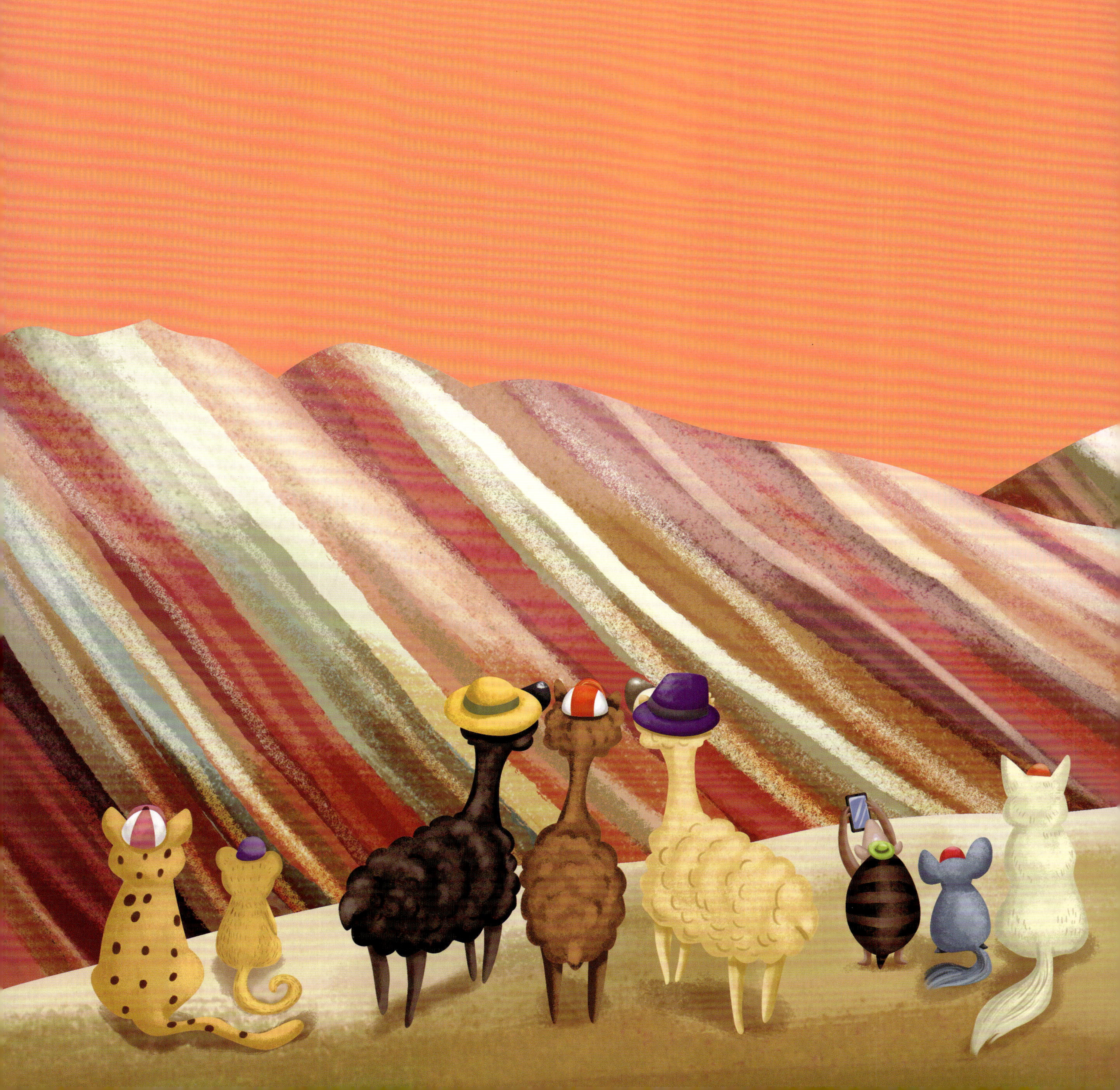

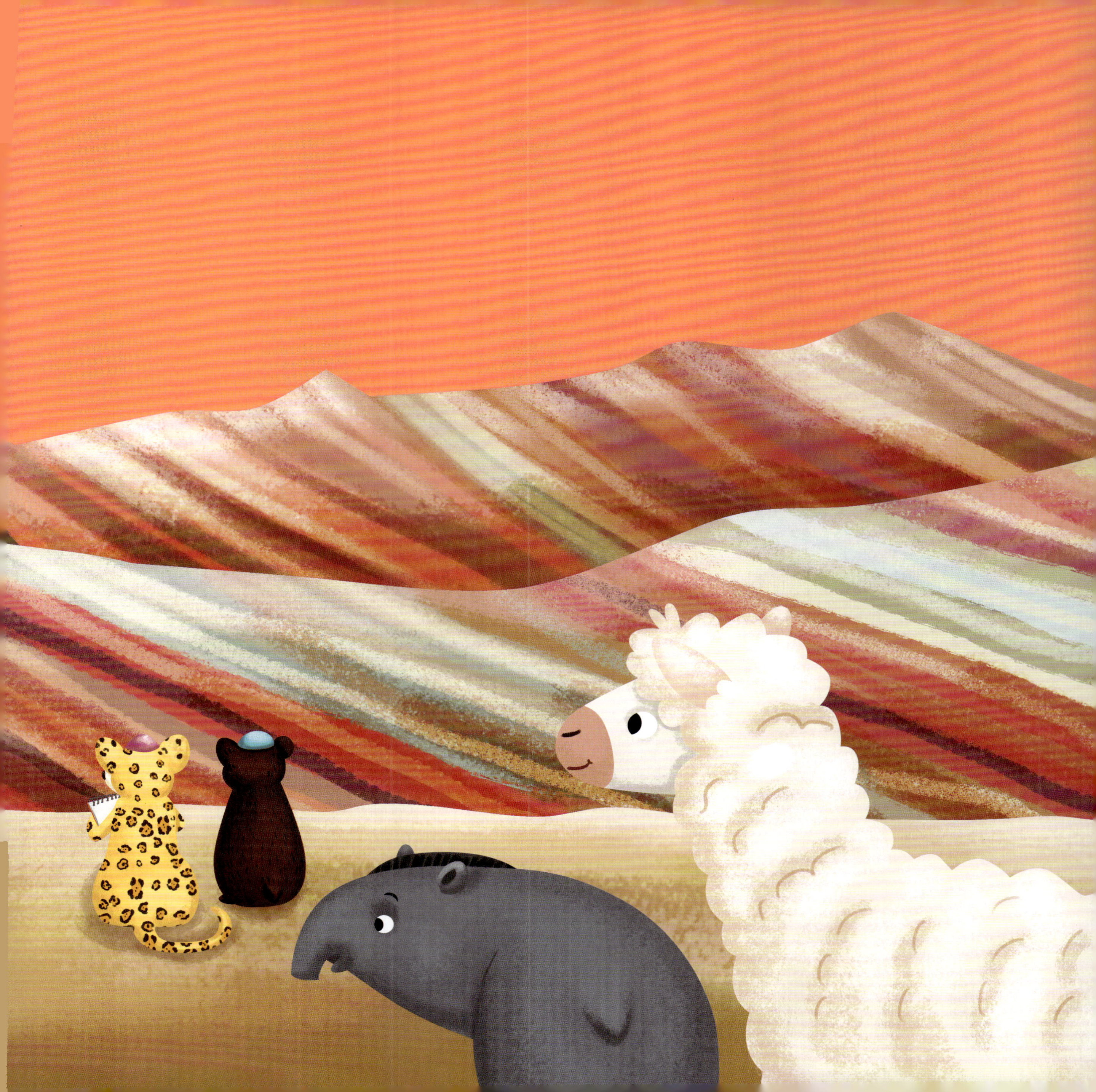

NOTES FOR PARENTS

It can be frustrating when you feel your child isn't listening to you, or when you're having to say something repeatedly. Learning to listen effectively is part of your child's social development, and even small children may deliberately ignore a request to see how a parent or carer might react.

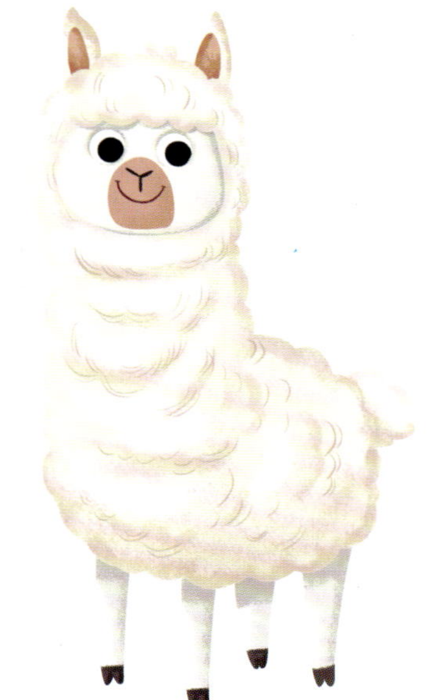

TIPS ON ENCOURAGING YOUR CHILD TO LISTEN

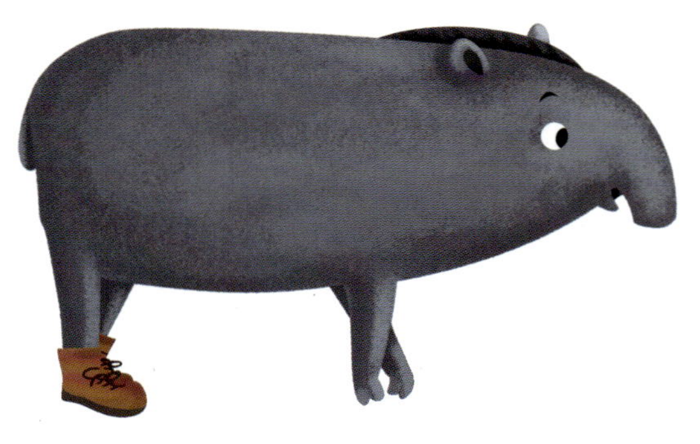

- Give your full attention when your child is trying to tell you something. They are far more likely to listen to you if you listen to them. This means stopping what you're doing, turning toward them or getting down to their level and making eye contact.

- Try to be concise in what you're saying, so your child doesn't tune out. Requests should be short, such as 'bedtime now' or 'shoes, please'.

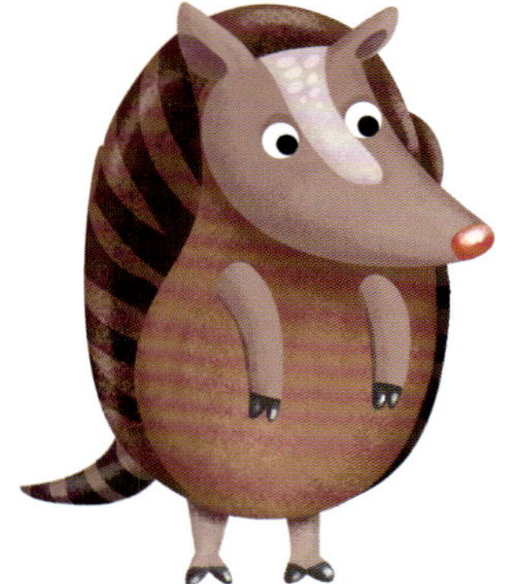

- If your child doesn't respond to your request, try to work out why they are not responding. It might help to try and see things from their point of view.

- Allow your child to feel they have power occasionally, for example by offering choices and allowing them to make decisions. This way, they are less likely to exert power in negative ways, such as ignoring you.

- Praise cooperation when they do something you've asked.